BOB SCOTT

The Birdwatcher's Calendar

A guide to birdwatching in Britain through the year

EBURY PRESS

to Ann, for more than just her binoculars and cameras!

Published by Ebury Press
National Magazine House
72 Broadwick Street
London W1V 2BP

First impression 1982

ISBN 0 85223 249 7

Illustrations by Tim Hayward, Trevor Boyer and
Colin Newman, by courtesy of Linden Artists Ltd, and by
Tony Maynard
Designed by Richard Garratt Design
Conceived and edited by Neil Curtis Publishing Services
Produced by Charles Herridge Ltd, Tower House,
Abbotsham, Devon
Typeset by Lens Typesetting, Bideford, Devon
Printed in Italy by New Interlitho SpA, Milan

Contents

The pleasures of birdwatching

Birdwatching as a hobby has great advantages over so many other pastimes. It is possible to enjoy it virtually anywhere and at any time. It is not necessary to make a special journey to some well-known bird reserve or to take part in a day's organized outing. The back garden, the local park, or the nearest farmland all support bird life – it is just a case of looking to see it. A train or coach journey can be enlivened by recording the different species seen although, at times, this can be frustrating because it is not possible to stop to check up on some particularly interesting bird that it wasn't possible to put a name to.

Don't try birdwatching on a car journey if you are driving and, if you are the passenger, remember not to distract the driver by pointing out the Kestrel hovering over the motorway embankment!

Most people watch birds in the countryside, however, and, before we go on to discuss the various items of equipment that can be useful, but are not essential for the amateur birdwatcher, there are two 'codes of practice' that should be borne in mind by all visitors to the country.

First, there is the 'Country Code' – prepared by the Countryside Commission, a statutory body concerned with the facilities for the enjoyment of the countryside:

1 Guard against all risk of fire
2 Fasten all gates
3 Keep dogs under proper control
4 Keep to the paths across farm land
5 Avoid damaging fences, hedges, and walls
6 Leave no litter
7 Safeguard water supplies
8 Protect wildlife, wild plants, and trees
9 Go carefully on country roads
10 Respect the life of the countryside.

Secondly, there is the 'Birdwatchers' Code of Conduct' – prepared and recommended by six different ornithological organizations including the Royal Society for the Protection of Birds (RSPB) and the British Trust for Ornithology (BTO):

1 The welfare of birds must come first
2 Habitat must be protected
3 Keep disturbance to birds and their habitat to a minimum
4 When you find a rare bird think carefully about whom you should tell
5 Do not harass rare migrants
6 Abide by the Bird Protection Acts at all times
7 Respect the right of landowners
8 Respect the rights of other people in the countryside
9 Make your records available to the local bird recorder
10 Behave abroad as you would when birdwatching at home.

What is a bird?

Modern birds occur in a bewildering variety exploiting every available habitat throughout the world. Generally, however, there are certain features that distinguish birds from all other living creatures although there are inevitable exceptions to every rule. For example, to say that birds enjoy the power of flight and that this separates them from other living creatures is quite a good definition, but there are obvious exceptions which most people are aware of. Ostriches, Kiwis, penguins, and several others have, for one reason or another, evolved to the stage where flight is no longer necessary for their survival; they can obtain their food and escape their enemies without it. Many insects have evolved highly developed flight capabilities which are, in many cases, superior to that of birds. And, of course, bats are very successful fliers. They are the only members of the mammal group to achieve this distinction although several gliding species exist.

Our modern bird has also retained some features of its reptilian ancestry. The legs and feet are covered with scales, and each toe ends in a well-formed claw, which, in many cases, has become highly developed into a talon. The newly hatched young of several species appear remarkably reptilian and are naked and helpless. The structure of a bird's jaw is also very similar to that of a reptile.

Let us attempt to define our bird by saying it is a warm-blooded vertebrate (ie it has a back bone), covered with feathers, which usually has the power of flight, lays eggs, and has a highly developed vocal ability. As we have seen, not all these features apply to birds alone. Mammals are also warm-blooded vertebrates; many insects fly; fishes and reptiles lay eggs, and man in particular has a highly developed vocal ability. If we examine the list carefully we find that only one feature is applicable to birds alone. Only birds are covered by feathers. This unique covering enables them to maintain their temperature and be very active; it enables them to fly (or swim, or balance) and thus find their food, to escape their predators, or to move to more hospitable areas in different seasons.

Among this wide variety of modern birds, one species survives which most clearly shows its relationship with the past. In the tropical forests of South America, particularly in the basin of the Amazon river, lives a very unusual bird, the Hoatzin (*Opisthocomus hoazin*) which seems to be remarkably similar to the ancient *Archaeopteryx*. Just as the long-extinct fossil bird would climb among the trees and glide to new feeding sites, so does the Hoatzin. Even more surprising are the behaviour and structure of the unfledged nestling. On the carpals, or shoulder joints, the young birds have well-developed claws which are capable of movement because of a specially developed muscle. Similar structures were present on *Archaeopteryx* and presumably served the same function. When well grown, but before flying, the young become highly adventurous, climbing among the vegetation using feet, bill, and claws all

Some of the many different types of British birds to show how they may differ in size and shape. From left to right: a typical wader; an eagle; a Blackbird; an owl; a goose; a Gannet; a Heron; a woodpecker; a Pheasant; and a Swallow.

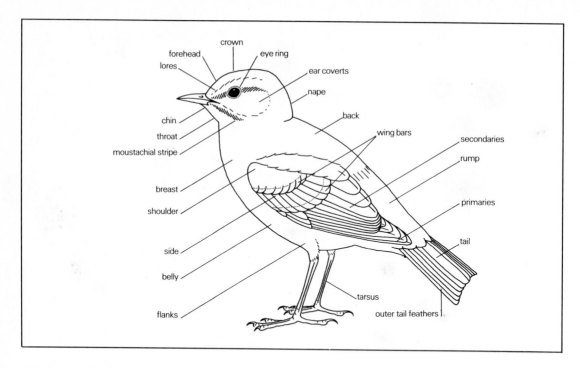

crown
forehead
eye ring
lores
ear coverts
nape
back
wing bars
secondaries
rump
chin
throat
moustachial stripe
primaries
breast
shoulder
tail
side
belly
tarsus
flanks
outer tail feathers

with equal ability and giving the birds great manoeuvrability. When danger threatens, they drop from the trees into the water below where, if they can avoid the waiting crocodiles, they swim and dive with great proficiency before using all their

The drawing shows the main features of a bird's appearance to note when you are describing it.

climbing powers to regain the overhanging vegetation.

The evolution of birds

The origins of birds as shown by fossil deposits must remain largely a matter of speculation – we must guess what the full picture may be when only certain parts of the jig-saw are available to us. Probably the best-known key piece in the whole story is the remains of *Archaeopteryx* which was an intermediate form between birds and reptiles and inhabited our world some 150 million years ago. This, of course, was well before man had evolved although small mammals had existed from some fifty million years earlier. These vast time periods are extremely difficult to comprehend when we consider that modern man, as a species, has only been on the Earth for some half-million years, and our modern calendar only deals with 2000 years.

In the distant past, about 225 million years ago, began a period that we call the Triassic which was to last for some thirty million years. During this period, when Britain was extremely arid and desert-like with some very salty lakes and rivers, a group of reptiles known as pseudosuchians inhabited the Earth and among them was *Euparkeria,* a member of the key group from which the birds were to evolve – here was just one further piece in the jig-saw.

The evolutionary experiment seems to have played with flight in two separate directions, both occurring at much the same time during the Jurassic period – both are well known. First, there were the pterodactyls, huge reptiles which were dominating the world at this time and had conquered the air by means of membranes stretched between their limbs to enable them to sustain gliding flight. The other experiment was the previously mentioned *Archaeopteryx*. The giant reptiles became extinct, disappearing around sixty-five million years ago, but *Archaeopteryx* was to succeed and diversify – animals with a covering of feathers had arrived.

Birds as we know them today were still 100 million years away but the *Euparkeria* type had successfully developed feathers from its covering of scales in an attempt to control its body temperature

It is thought that modern birds may have evolved from a reptile such as Euparkeria *(top) which lived about 225 million years ago; the well-known fossil of* Archaeopteryx *shows characteristics of birds and reptiles including feathers and teeth; the South America Hoatzin seems to be remarkably similar to* Archaeopteryx. · *Finally, a typical modern bird – a Blackbird.*

and, just as the pterodactyls had experimented with gliding, so could *Archaeopteryx,* using the feathers attached to its fore limbs. From this humble beginning the diversity of the bird life that inhabits the world today, perhaps 8600 species, has evolved. Many experiments along the way have resulted in dead ends with no subsequent development, including giant flightless birds or huge tern–like species, appearing and disappearing as time passed. Most modern families of birds evolved during the period between sixty-five and ten million years ago, a huge span of time that enabled the evolutionary experiment to develop to the present-day position. The change continues, of course, but we are only able to witness such a short interval of time that major changes do not become obvious and we see an apparently unchanging natural world.

In an attempt to place the evolution story into perspective, the 4500 million years of the Earth's existence has been likened to the twenty-four hours of a day, with the world appearing at the beginning of the day; in this context, *Archaeopteryx* appeared at the start of the last hour and man has evolved with only about twelve seconds to go!

The naming of birds

Each of the 8600 different types of birds known throughout the world has a name. In western Europe most birds have English names as well as names in the other European languages. For many birds in South America or on the Pacific islands, for example, no generally accepted English names exist and authors of books on these regions often need to invent their own names. But each different type of bird has also been given its own unique scientific name. A birdwatcher in Bulgaria who speaks no English will refer to birds by the same scientific names as the English birdwatcher who speaks no Bulgarian does. The scientific name of a bird is made up of two words which, in this book, are written in italics and follow the English names. These scientific names are international. The scientific name of the bird which, in English, we call the Kestrel is *Falco tinnunculus,* and this name would be the same throughout the world even though its common name would be different in various languages. For example, Swedish: Tornfalk; French: Faucon crecerelle; Afrikaans: Ngami-rooivalkie; German: Turmfalke; Spanish: Cernicalo vulgar; Dutch: Torenvalk.

This system of scientific names is referred to as the binomial system and dates from 1758 when a Swedish naturalist called Carl Linnaeus published a book entitled *Systema Natura* in which all living things were catalogued and given two names in Latin, the international language of the time. The first of the two names indicated animal and plant relationships and closely related types had the same name known as the genus. The second name indicated the species and, therefore, the differences between animals (or plants).

The two names together give a unique combination that will separate a species from any other, any-where in the world. If we return to our Kestrel, *Falco* is the genus, a name shared by the Hobby, Peregrine, and Merlin, all falcons, but distinctly separate species, so that: Kestrel *(Falco tinnunculus);* Hobby *(Falco subbuteo);* Peregrine *(Falco peregrinus);* Merlin *(Falco columbarius).*

The Sparrowhawk, on the other hand, is a bird of prey like the Kestrel but it is clearly a member of a different group because of its striking structural and behavioural differences so that it is given the name *Accipiter nisus.* It is, however, a very close relative of the Goshawk and to show this relationship, Goshawk *(Accipiter gentilis).* When books continue to refer to species in the same genus, the generic name is frequently abbreviated. If we now wish to mention the closely related south-east European member of this group, we can write: Levant Sparrowhawk *(A. brevipes)* indicating that we are still referring to the genus *Accipiter.*

Occasionally, a completely new species of bird is discovered. It may be from some less well-known part of the world, such as the forested highlands of Equatorial New Guinea or the hinterland of Borneo, or even rediscovered in the bottom of a dusty museum drawer. The first person to publish details of the find, together with a description of the bird, is known as the author and must give the new bird two names. The first will be the genus to which it belongs and the second will be its own unique name for the species. Very recently, a paper was published by Louette and Benson in the *Bulletin of the British Ornithologists' Club* in which they described a new species of weaver, a group of African finches from the swamps of Zaire. They named the bird *Ploceus ruweti* and its full reference with authors becomes: *Ploceus ruweti* Louette & Benson, 1982. As yet the bird has no English name.

'British' birds

For a bird to be claimed as 'British', it must have been recorded wild in the British Isles. To assess these occurrences and to compile the official 'British List', the British Ornithologists' Union, the senior ornithological society in Britain, has a records committee which meets at regular intervals and presents reports on recent changes. In 1971 the committee published the definitive list and status of all British species in a book entitled *The Status of Birds in Britain and Ireland* and, since that publication, it has updated the information with regular reports in the BOU's journal, *Ibis*. The total number of species on the British list is now over 520, and these are separated into four distinct categories:

1 species which have been recorded in an apparently wild state in Britain or Ireland at least once within the last fifty years;

2 species which have been recorded in an apparently wild state in Britain or Ireland at least once, but not within the last fifty years;

3 species which, although originally introduced by man, have now established a regular feral breeding stock which apparently maintains itself without necessary recourse to further introduction;

4 species which have been recorded within the last fifty years and would otherwise appear in category 1 except that (a) there is a reasonable doubt they have ever occurred in a wild state, or (b) they have certainly arrived with ship–assistance, or (c) they have only ever been found dead on the tide line; also species which would otherwise appear in category 3 except that their feral populations may or may not be self-supporting.

In addition to the official list of British birds, the journal *British Birds* has a rarities committee that assesses the occurrences in Britain of the rarer species. In conjunction with the Irish Records Panel and the Northern Ireland Bird Records Committee, they publish an annual report which details the occurrences and any change in status of our rarer visitors. An observer who encounters a species that comes within the jurisdiction of the committee is asked to submit full details of the record, including a description of the bird, for the committee's consideration. For extreme rarities it is obviously advisable, whenever possible, to obtain confirmation of the record from an experienced birdwatcher.

The following description is an example of the supporting evidence necessary to claim a rare bird, and is taken from the author's diary and concerns a male Ring-necked Duck *(Aythya collaris)*, a rare visitor from North America seen at the Llys-y-fran reservoir in Dyfed on 15 September 1978:

On arrival at the reservoir at 1045 hrs a single duck was located at some distance – the bird could not be immediately identified and there were no other wildfowl present for comparative purposes.

During the following 40-50 minutes the bird was watched at ranges down to 50 metres through 8× and 10× binoculars and a 20-40× telescope. The day was bright and sunny, although at times the bird was viewed against the light in sun-reflecting water.

The best views were obtained looking angled down at the bird from the bank at its closest point of some 50 metres. At no time did it dive, although regularly twisting and turning its neck to watch passing Buzzards. On the one occasion that the bird flew it was unfortunately directly towards the sun and no details could be seen, although some form of pale/white wing bar was obviously present.

The bird was clearly an Aythya of the Tufted/Scaup type – but the bird did not jizz correctly for either species and consequently much time was spent in examining the bird and taking notes. It was only when comparing these notes with field guides at a later stage that it became obvious that the bird was a Ring-necked Duck – a species new to the observer.

Superficially the bird was a male Tufted Duck but differed in not having an obvious tuft of feathers, in having a high-peaked head, in having dusky greyish (not white) sides to the body (flanks), the off-white flanks coming up to form a point or peak in front of the folded wings, the slate-coloured bill having a black nail and two white bands, one immediately behind the nail, the other at the base. On one occasion, when the bird drifted sideways to the wind, a small area of loose tuft-like feathers was apparent on the back of the crown – at other times the head looked completely smooth. The eye was a bright golden-yellow and the head showed a distinct purple sheen. Breast, back, tail, and under tail coverts were a uniform black. The primaries of the folded wing were showing lighter areas contrasting with the black back.

The record was accepted by the Rarities Committee and appeared in the 'Report on rare birds in Great Britain in 1978' published in the November 1979 issue of the journal *British Birds*.

Bird families and way of life

The diversity of bird life is truly overwhelming ranging as it does from the smallest insect-eating warbler, through the scavenging crow and predatory eagle, to the majestic swan. The table below lists the different families of British birds in evolutionary order giving the scientific name of the group as well as the common names.

Each of these families has evolved to exploit the various habitats but, within each group, there are more subtle differences – the specific differences that separate each individual into the different species that, in very small ways, behave differently and avoid direct competition with their closest relatives.

GAVIIDAE	divers
PODICIPEDIDAE	grebes
PROCELLARIIDAE	shearwaters
HYDROBATIDAE	petrels
SULIDAE	gannets
PHALACROCORACIDAE	cormorants
ARDEIDAE	herons
ANATIDAE	wildfowl
ACCIPITRIDAE	hawks, eagles
PANDIONIDAE	ospreys
FALCONIDAE	falcons
TETRAONIDAE	grouse
PHASIANIDAE	pheasants
RALLIDAE	crakes, rails, coots
HAEMATOPODIDAE	oystercatchers
RECURVIROSTRIDAE	avocets
BURHINIDAE	stone curlews
CHARADRIIDAE	plovers
SCOLOPACIDAE	sandpipers, snipe
STERCORARIIDAE	skuas
LARIDAE	gulls
STERNIDAE	terns
ALCIDAE	auks
COLUMBIDAE	pigeons
CUCULIDAE	cuckoos
TYTONIDAE	barn owls
STRIGIDAE	owls
CAPRIMULGIDAE	nightjars
APODIDAE	swifts
ALCEDINIDAE	kingfishers
PICIDAE	woodpeckers
ALAUDIDAE	larks
HIRUNDINIDAE	swallows
MOTACILLIDAE	wagtails, pipits
CINCLIDAE	dippers
TROGLODYTIDAE	wrens
PRUNELLIDAE	dunnocks
TURDIDAE	thrushes
SYLVIIDAE	warblers
MUSCICAPIDAE	flycatchers
TIMALIIDAE	reedlings
AEGITHALIDAE	long-tailed tits
PARIDAE	tits
SITTIDAE	nuthatches
CERTHIIDAE	treecreepers
LANIIDAE	shrikes
CORVIDAE	crows
STURNIDAE	starlings
PASSERIDAE	sparrows
FRINGILLIDAE	finches
EMBERIZIDAE	buntings

A close look at some common British species from a familiar family will provide a useful selection of examples to illustrate the point: the Fringillidae, or finches, and five different species.

Chaffinch *(Fringilla coelebs)* – one of the commonest British birds which, as a ground feeder, exploits a very wide diet. It is a non-specialist, taking advantage of any available food supply from the beech mast crop in years of superabundance, to the spilt grain around animal feeding sites, or the open farmland or recently sown fields. For breeding purposes it requires deciduous woodland, or parkland and hedgerow containing mature trees for suitable song posts.

Hawfinch *(Coccothraustes coccothraustes)* – a rather shy bird that favours open woodland and parks, and has a particular liking for orchards. The extremely large bill enables the bird to tackle such food items as cherry stones which are well beyond the capabilities of other finches. The inside of the bill is ridged to help it maintain a firm grip, while the skull is strengthened and modified to house the powerful jaw muscles. The Hawfinch is largely confined to the trees but it will feed on the ground in the autumn and winter when the fruit has fallen.

Goldfinch *(Carduelis carduelis)* – an agile feeder which clings to the tops of low-growing vegetation where the very pointed bill is ideally suited for extracting the seeds from thistles and teasels. It is very much a bird of open waste ground or the scrub edge of a woodland site.

Bullfinch *(Pyrrhula pyrrhula)* – it is extremely rare for this species to venture on to the ground and it keeps to the undergrowth in woods or in dense shrubberies or unmaintained hedgerows. The short, rounded, stubby bill is ideally suited to exploit its main diet of buds and berries.

Crossbill *(Loxia curvirostra)* – one of the most specialized of the finches, dependent upon the conifer woods where the specially developed crossed mandibles enable the bird to extract the seeds from cones. Even here there is specific variation for, in Europe, there are three species of crossbills and, in descending order of bill size, they have preferences for different cones: Parrot Crossbill *(L. pytyopsittacus)* – pine cones; Crossbill *(L. curvirostra)* – spruce cones; Two-barred Crossbill *(L. leucoptera)* – larch cones.

A year in the life of a bird

The annual cycle in the life of any bird species is unique. Even closely related species show differences as each slots into its own particular place in the environment. To give details of the wide range of individual annual cycles would take millions of words in thousands of books. Indeed, relatively recent monographs have devoted some 300 pages to the Wren *(Troglodytes troglodytes)*, 280 to the Dotterel *(Charadrius morinellus)*, 190 to the Buzzard *(Buteo buteo)*, over 400 to the Peregrine *(Falco peregrinus)*, and 330 to the Gannet *(Sula bassana)*. Such works are by no means exhaustive as more knowledge is gained from further observations and as bird populations change and behaviour alters in response to climatic variations, altering food supply, available nesting sites, and so on.

The following necessarily rather brief summaries of the annual cycles of two very different species of British birds will give some indication of the wide range of life-styles.

A Blackbird year

The Blackbird *(Turdus merula)* can be seen in Britain throughout the year. Generally, it is considered to be a resident and one of the most numerous of British nesting land birds with an estimated population in excess of seven million pairs.

We start the Blackbird's year in late July/early August. The last of the young to be reared in that year are now independent and have shed their fluffy,

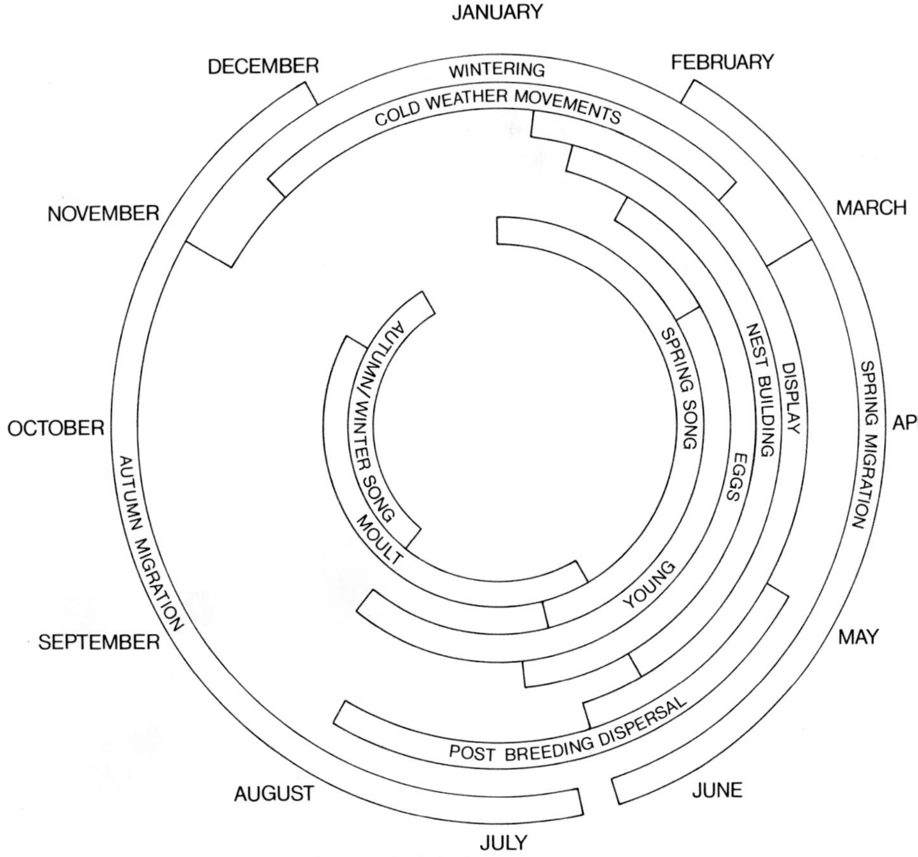

The chart shows the times of the year during which birds carry out important activities such as moulting or display. You will notice that many of these activities overlap.

Birds' feathers may become worn and damaged through the year and must be changed. Some birds cannot fly when this takes place while others become less manoeuvrable and easy prey for predators. For any particular species the moult takes place in a particular order.

downy body plumage with which they left the nest and have moulted into the more practical, stiffer feathering that will take them through the winter and next year's breeding season. The wing and tail feathers are not changed; they are to remain with the bird because a young, inexperienced fledgling just out of the nest could not afford to be incapacitated by impaired flight during its early formative months. The adults must change all their feathers. They have become worn, bleached, and broken during the hard work of the summer months building nests and feeding young. To survive the coming winter they must be in perfect condition. Over a period of about four to five weeks, the feathers are slowly changed. One feather drops and the new one starts to grow before the next feather drops. The bird is still able to fly but it is less manoeuvrable. The birds become quiet and they skulk. They are easier prey for predators and the process of moulting places extreme pressure on the physical condition of the bird.

With moulting complete, there is some dispersal from the breeding grounds. The adult males remain but the females and young of that year move away although they rarely move far. Often they form small flocks which assemble at available food supplies such as berry hedges or damp grass meadows where they can obtain insects and worms from the soil. At this time of the year, the young males can be distinguished from the adult males by the all-dark (not yellow) bills and the markedly brown, rather than black wing feathers.

As the autumn progresses, colder weather in northern and eastern Europe forces Continental Blackbirds to move west and south to seek a milder climate. Throughout October and November, particularly on the east coast of England and Scotland, large-scale thrush migrations can take place with Blackbirds figuring predominantly among them. Mortality at this time is high, but to remain on those distant breeding grounds throughout the winter is certain death and the risk of such a long journey is much lower. Many of these Continental Blackbirds just pass through Britain to an eventual wintering

The 'mutual penguin dance' of the Great Crested Grebe is one of the most exciting events of spring for the British birdwatcher. Nearby a Tree Pipit engages in its descending song flight.

Dunlin and Redshank feed on the mud of an estuary while an acrobatic Greenfinch exploits a peanut bag together with a typical birdtable species, the Blue Tit.

Some typical nest sites. From left to right: a Guillemot simply lays its egg on the ledge of a sea cliff; a House Martin constructs its mud nest under the eaves of a house while a Robin finds a secluded spot in a hedge bank; a Lapwing nests on the ground and, when threatened, the parent may engage in an elaborate display to distract the attention of any potential predator away from the nest.

ground in western France or Spain, but large numbers remain to swell the British population.

Throughout the winter, these two groups, the British breeding birds and the Continental visitors, readily mix, jointly exploiting any food supply that is available and often intermingling with other winter thrushes in large communal roosts. As well as killing many birds, severe winter weather will often force the foreign birds to move further south but the British stock is more likely to remain.

Before the winter is over, the British males are again establishing their breeding territories, and the young birds must carve out sites for the first time. They will occupy territories that have become vacant as the result of winter casualties, or establish a site in direct competition with an occupying bird. A rather ritualized chasing and fighting procedure takes place with the contesting males running backwards and forwards around the boundary of the disputed territory occasionally coming face to face and flying upwards in what appears to be vicious fighting but it is usually more bluff and posturing than real combat. As this territorial conflict proceeds and the spring song develops, the foreign visitors have rather quietly slipped away during a March night to head back in an easterly direction and leave only the British resident birds.

The territory has been established, pairs have been formed, and nest site selection and building begin. In a normal season, a pair of Blackbirds may have two three, or, exceptionally, four broods. Each clutch will consist of four or five eggs, but this potential of twenty young reared is rarely realized because egg loss and mortality in various forms all take their toll. To achieve a stable population it is only necessary to rear enough young to replace the adult losses, so perhaps only one or two of the possible twenty eggs will grow into breeding adult Blackbirds.

A Common Tern year

As a complete contrast, the annual cycle of the Common Tern *(Sterna hirundo)* refers to a species that is a summer visitor only to British shores, spending the winter months off the West African coast. As a breeding bird, it is mainly confined to coastal localities but small colonies do exist on islands at inland water sites. In spring, the birds leave their wintering grounds and follow a migration route that takes them along the Atlantic seaboard until they reach British waters in mid-April. By the end of the month many birds have arrived on their nesting grounds and started their ritualized displays that

accompany pairing and breeding. Other birds have still to arrive and many passage birds are still flying off the British coast on their way to more northern sites.

The breeding pairs are established upon the arrival of the Terns at the nesting grounds. The males present the females with fish in a feeding ceremony that continues throughout the incubation of the eggs which is shared by both birds. No real nest is constructed and the two or three well-camouflaged eggs are laid in a shallow scrape in the ground. Only a single breeding attempt is made each year, although lost eggs will be replaced if the season is not too far advanced.

By late July the young, which are active within a few days of hatching, have fledged and the immatures and adults assemble at coastal areas where food supplies are abundant. As Blackbirds do, the adult Common Terns undertake a post-breeding moult to replace the worn feathers, but there are two different factors that are most important. Firstly, the Tern will have to fly to Africa and this cannot be safely accomplished if the flight feathers are worn or damaged. Secondly, the Common Tern relies upon its flying ability to obtain food by diving into the sea for small fishes. To some extent, these criteria are in conflict because the quicker the bird moults the better it is equipped for migration but it can feed less effectively. Therefore, a partial moult is undertaken near the breeding grounds, when nearly half the flight feathers are renewed, but then the moult is 'arrested' to be completed when the bird arrives at the wintering quarters. The ability to feed is only slightly impaired, and some fresh flight feathers are available for the journey.

Common Terns do not breed until they are two years old, and the young remain on the wintering

Although they will still keep close to the parent bird, young ducklings (left) are able to feed themselves from a very early age while a Songthrush adult may still be feeding its young when they are out of the nest and almost as big as the parent.

grounds throughout the first summer of their lives, only returning northwards when their second winter in African waters is past.

Several closely related species have quite significant differences in their annual cycles. The Willow Warbler *(Phylloscopus trochilus)* has a spring and autumn moult, preceeding each of its migrations; the Chiffchaff *(P. collybita),* which winters further north, only moults in the autumn. The Marsh Tit *(Parus palustris)* nests in natural holes in woodland trees; the Willow Tit *(P. montanus)* excavates its own nesting hole from the rotten wood in dead stumps. Short-eared Owls *(Asio flammeus)* nest on the ground in open country and are frequently to be seen hunting in daylight; the Long-eared Owl *(A. otus)* is a strictly nocturnal species which chooses the abandoned nest of a Crow in a woodland setting for its nest site. The Mistle Thrush *(Turdus viscivorus)* will start nesting very early in the season and defends its nest with bold attacks against potential predators; the Song Thrush *(T. philomelos)* nests much later in the year and is unlikely to offer any defence. The Tree Pipit *(Anthus trivialis)* is a summer visitor to Britain; the Meadow Pipit *(A. pratensis)* is present throughout the year.

The list is virtually inexhaustible, each species varies its annual cycle according to the pattern that has evolved over thousands of years and the subtle variations prevent one species entering into direct conflict with another.

Birds and their environment

If you examine the illustrations of birds in this or any other bird book you will easily see the great variety of bird form and structure. Each different type has evolved to exploit some particular habitat or food source. In Britain alone, birds can be encountered everywhere, and this is perhaps one of the greatest beauties of birdwatching as a hobby – wherever you are there are birds to watch, listen to, or study. A boat far offshore will attract such highly marine species as shearwaters or petrels; close inshore the gulls and terns are more in evidence; while on the beaches the species to be encountered will depend upon whether the habitat is sand, mud, rocks, cliffs, or harbours. In such a relatively short journey from beach to open ocean we have seen a wide range of habitats and a wide range of species, each exploiting its own niche.

On the sea cliffs the Fulmars *(Fulmarus glacialis)* nest, and glide past on stiff outstretched wings in apparently effortless flight. The aerodynamics of these birds enable them to use each updraught of air to stay on the wing, arriving and departing from the nesting ledge with the utmost ease. In the harbours, the gulls forage for scraps, circling over the water's edge or around the boats like ever-watchful vultures, ready

The great variety in the size, shape, and structure of birds' bills enables them to exploit many different food supplies. From top to bottom: an eagle's bill for tearing up prey; a long, curved bill of a Curlew for extracting food from the deep mud of an estuary; a heavy Hawfinch bill for cracking cherry stones; a warbler's finely pointed bill for catching insects.

The legs and feet of birds, too, have evolved to suit their different lifestyles. A duck's webbed foot enables it to paddle through the water. A flycatcher's foot is typical of perching birds. The powerful talons of an Osprey enable it to seize and carry slippery fishes. A Moorhen can be just as at home among reeds, on dry land, or on the water.

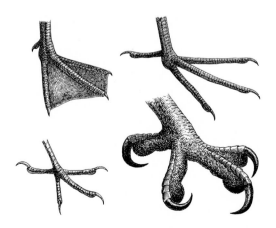

to descend en masse as any new food source becomes available. A returning fishing boat is a signal for a great assembly and welcoming committee, the birds flying out to greet this new food supply as it enters the harbour mouth.

Well camouflaged among the seaweed-covered rocks is a mixed flock of Turnstones *(Arenaria interpres)* and Purple Sandpipers *(Calidris maritima)*, their rather strong, stout bills searching and probing among the rocks for the small marine crustaceans marooned there by the retreating tide and now awaiting the return of the water. In keeping with its name, the Turnstone flicks over small stones or clumps of weed to search beneath them. The more open beaches of sand and mud provide a food source for the probing waders, the long-billed Curlew *(Numenius arquata)* on the softest mud, searching for the deepest food; the shorter-billed plovers on the sandier, stonier beaches where they pick from the surface to exploit an altogether different food supply. In the shallow waters close inshore, the various species of tern are plunge-diving for small fishes or sand eels which swim in large shoals enjoying the warmer water or perhaps driven there by the larger predatory fishes from further out to sea. Bigger fishes themselves provide a food source for the larger diving birds, the Cormorants *(Phalacrocorax carbo)* and Shags *(P. aristotelis)* which dive from a swimming position, or the Gannets *(Sula bassana)* which plunge-dive from a considerable height. And finally, on this brief journey from shore to ocean, the shearwaters skim the surface of the waves, making use of the slightest air currents under their long, narrow, gliding wings. Out here they feed on the marine shrimps that support so much of the wildlife in the open oceans of the world.

Just as with the sea, then so with the land. The birds that inhabit the densest woodlands have evolved to exploit the food supply and nest sites that this habitat presents. The woodpeckers are very dependent upon trees, while the larks and pipits require open ground. Similarly, the wagtails look for open country but they also need water close by, while the Dipper *(Cinclus cinclus)* looks for fast-flowing streams, and the Dartford Warbler *(Sylvia undata)* needs the gorse- and heather-clad heathland. Each habitat has its own unique fauna, and each group of birds has developed to exploit these habitats.

Where to watch birds

Birdwatchers have a great advantage when it comes to pursuing their hobby; there are birds everywhere from the wildest, bleakest mountain side to the noisiest, most densely populated town square. There is one golden rule, however; you must obtain permission before attempting to gain access to any land unless it is a public place. There appears to be an ever-increasing tendency for birdwatchers to head towards the 'honeypots' of the bird world, those reserves and other sites which have acquired a reputation for the variety and rarity of the bird species present. In some ways, this is a great pity for sites on everyone's doorstep can be just as interesting, and it is just a case of discovering them.

To discover a new birdwatching haunt there is no better guide than the Ordnance Survey 1:50 000 series of maps. Throughout this book the reference number of the map has been given on which the site mentioned can be located. A close examination of your local map could well lead you to an undiscovered block of woodland, a small marsh or pond, or even an unexplored river-side walk. Start by looking for public footpaths or areas where access is assured. Usually permission must be obtained to enter woods or visit reservoirs. Unless there is some particular reason, most landowners and authorities are agreeable, if approached politely and reasonably, to allow access for birdwatching. It is the unagreed entry on to private land that may well result in a birdwatching ban.

Discovering these new birdwatching haunts and the unexpected species on your own 'patch' is one of the most exciting moments of the hobby. Finding a quite common species, too, in an unlikely situation near your own home can be just as rewarding as the rarest bird in a known site many kilometres away. Scattered throughout Britain are 'traditional' sites, sites which have rightly acquired a reputation for their bird and wildlife interest. Many of these sites are mentioned through the pages of this book, but remember that a reference to a site here does not indicate that there is free or open access to the locality. Many are reserves owned and managed by the various conservation bodies and a large number will have restricted access in some form or other. Details of visiting arrangements *must* be obtained before planning a trip.

Most reserves in Britain come under the auspices of three organizations: the Nature Conservancy Council which controls the National Nature Reserves; the Royal Society for the Protection of Birds which manages nationally important sites; and the county nature conservation trusts which, under their umbrella body, the Royal Society for Nature Conservation, operate a system of county reserves many of which are of great interest to the birdwatcher. All these organizations provide details for visiting their reserves, and their addresses are given at the end of the book.

Around the British coastline are some fifteen bird observatories based on particularly important bird migration sites. They operate a programme of bird studies and offer hostel-type accommodation to visitors. Each observatory is based at a site that can be especially exciting at certain times of the year and, although each is operated on an independent basis, they all co-operate through their co-ordinating body, the Bird Observatories Council.

Bird habitats

Each of the different habitats mentioned throughout this book is exploited by different bird species in different ways. Some birds are highly adaptable and can be found in many different sites. The Jackdaw is a great opportunist and can be encountered nesting on sea cliffs among the colonial Guillemots and Kittiwakes; on town buildings with the feral pigeons and Starlings; and in woodland sites with the Stock Doves and Tawny Owls. In complete contrast, species such as the Dartford Warbler and Crested Tit are confined to the heaths of southern England and pine forests of Scotland's Spey Valley respectively.

WOODLAND

This is the natural habitat of many of our familiar garden birds. Formerly, the various types of woodland cover were present over much of the British countryside but, as the activities of man increased, the woodland began to disappear and become fragmented. Many of the modern woods are man made, planted on a commercial basis and consisting of a solid block of a single species, lacking the diversity that will ensure a variety of bird life. It is the mixed, 'untidy' wood with the clearings and rides, scrub cover and undergrowth, standing and fallen dead timber, that provides the richest mixture of birds.

The woodland birdwatcher's ears are at least as important as the eyes. It is often a case of 'bird-

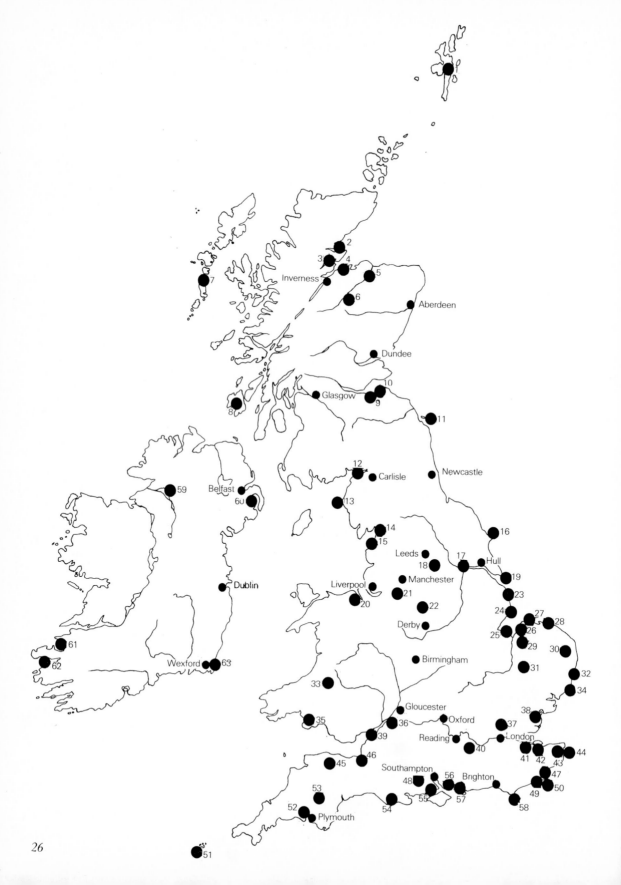

A map of the British Isles showing a selection of many of the important traditional birdwatching sites mentioned in this book:

listening' rather than watching! Vision is restricted by the vegetation but, in the spring and early summer, the bird song is overwhelming and, in a site with a high bird density, almost deafening. In spring and summer it is best to stand quietly at a point where you can see across a clearing or along a ride and with your back against a tree. Then watch for movement in the vegetation. Searching the cover through binoculars is likely to be totally unrewarding; watch for movement with the naked eye and then focus the binoculars on the spot. With patience, even the most skulking singing bird will disclose its presence by moving. Quietly sitting in a wood can be highly rewarding. In the canopy the Blue Tits, Goldcrests, and Willow Warblers are feeding on the outermost leaves; on the branches are the Nuthatches and Great Tits; on the trunk the woodpeckers and Treecreeper; and in the scrub the Whitethroats and Nightingales. Each of the woodland species inhabits its own niche.

Winter watching in woodland is less varied, for the summer migrants have departed, but it is a little easier because the leaves have fallen and many species have gathered into mixed flocks. This is particularly true of the tits. In the winter you can be a little more active, and walk along the woodland rides, still listening, but also watching for the first sign of a foraging, feeding party of birds. Once you have found one, you should try to get in front of the general movement of the flock and then stand quietly as the birds work their way past. The continual high-pitched contact calls enable all the individuals to maintain themselves as a unit. These mixed tit flocks are often joined by Treecreepers, Nuthatches, Goldcrests, wintering Blackcaps, and even the occasional Lesser Spotted Woodpecker.

COAST

Britain's very varied coastline provides a rich ornithological backcloth for the birdwatcher. The high sea cliffs and rocky off-shore islands hold large numbers of nesting sea birds from the rich North Atlantic feeding grounds. Sea cliffs that are devoid of bird interest for most of the winter months come alive during April and May as the ledges fill with row upon row of Guillemots or soaring, swirling Kittiwakes and sedately gliding Fulmars. The greatest density of sea bird colonies is in the north and west and, unfortunately, many of them are on the off-shore islands with difficult access. The few mainland sites rarely provide good views and the birdwatcher must take extreme care when watching from cliff tops. Never climb over any cliff-top fences and only watch from observation posts where these are provided. No specialized techniques are required because most sea birds feel safe even when viewed from above, and watching from the cliff tops rarely disrupts any activity among the colony. Even on an apparently uniform cliff face, different species are in different areas, with Shags on the rocks at sea-level, Guillemots lining the ledges, and Razorbills tucked into the crevices and beneath the overhangs.

Elsewhere on the coast, the open mudflats, tidal marshes, and shingle beaches attract a completely different variety of birds which require a very different viewing technique. These birds are wary, easy to disturb, and will never allow close approach. This is where the spotting 'scope comes into its own, and where the birdwatcher should allow the birds to come to him by letting the tide do the work. If the sea cliffs are a site for summer watching, the open beaches are a winter habitat. Vast numbers of northern waders and wildfowl move south for the winter months and exploit the rich food supply found in the coastal marshes that are flooded twice daily by the incoming tide. No matter how cold the winter weather, this food supply is never frozen and some of the larger estuaries provide a winter home for hundreds of thousands of birds.

MARSH

A steady programme of drainage and reclamation has reduced the once vast marshes of eastern and southern England until the present-day reed beds, swamps, and flooded meadows are small isolated patches in contrast to their former abundance. Most of the sites that remain are protected as nature reserves and the highly specialized species that inhabit these areas are now safeguarded. Many of the species are rare because the habitat is rare. The Bitterns and Marsh Harriers of the reed beds, the Avocets of the shallow lagoons, and the Black-tailed Godwits and Ruff of the flooded meadows will never be widespread.

Although the birds are rare, observing them is easy. Many of the marshland reserves have excellent visitor facilities with observation hides and covered approaches that enable the birds to be watched at close quarters with no disturbance. Viewing birds from hides would appear to be easy birdwatching, but one or two rules should be closely observed. Keep quiet. The birds are used to the hide and

perhaps even to a small amount of movement that they can see through the viewing slots, but a sudden noise can easily frighten them away. Never wave your arm through the viewing slot. It is very easy and tempting to point out a bird to your companion sitting next to you by thrusting out your arm but then the birds all take flight. Similarly, do not suddenly point a telescope through the slot. Remember not to bang the hide door when you leave and try not to move across between an open door and a viewing slot because the birds outside will see the movement against the light.

HEATHS

Heaths are fragmented and specialized habitats and are among the most difficult and least productive for the birdwatcher. The bird population is low and, in the winter months, there are few birds at all. There are not many areas where birds occur in any numbers. Usually there is just a small population which is widespread among the heather and gorse. The birdwatcher can but walk the paths and tracks hoping to make contact with some of the exciting species that can be located. This is very much a southern habitat and home of the rare Hobby and Dartford Warbler, as well as the more familiar Stonechat and Yellowhammer. A dusk visit could well reveal the presence of a churring Nightjar or reeling song of a Grasshopper Warbler; but the season is short for, by late July, the heaths are deserted and hold little of ornithological interest until the following May.

UPLANDS

The mountains and moorlands are the northern equivalents of the southern heaths. The bird populations are exciting and in many cases very rare, but they are also very sparse in their distribution and virtually absent in the winter months. The areas involved are huge, ranging from the high peaks of north Wales, with their nesting Choughs, to the rugged magnificence of the Scottish Highlands with the soaring Golden Eagles. This is birdwatching for the expert, not the terrain for the casual visitor or holidaymaker to enter in a search for birds. To leave the well-trodden paths and tracks requires specialist equipment and, for most birdwatchers visiting these regions, the advice must be to keep to the main trackways, and have stout footwear and plenty of warm and waterproof clothing.

LAKES and RIVERS

Water attracts a wide range of bird life, and sites as separate as a southern gravel pit or Scottish loch hold great interest for the birdwatcher. As the number of water areas grows as a result of commercial needs, and rivers are cleaned and improved, the bird-watcher has more and more sites to visit. Coupled with this increase in sites there has been an increase in bird populations, with breeding Great Crested Grebes and Tufted Ducks now common and widespread.

River-side birdwatching can be one of the most pleasant and relaxing of pastimes. Many rivers have public walks along their banks so that by sitting quietly in a position with a view you may well see the flash of blue from a flying Kingfisher or the movement in the reeds that discloses a nesting Little Grebe. Often the birds in these situations have become accustomed to the presence of fishermen and walkers and, as a result, they will allow close approach. Outside the breeding season the seeds of the river-side alders will attract mixed flocks of Redpolls and Siskins feeding with the agility of tits.

The larger areas of open water can be worth visiting throughout the year. There may be fishing Ospreys on a Scottish loch, Red-breasted Mergansers on an Irish lough, Goosanders on a northern lake, or Little Ringed Plovers on a southern gravel pit – all attracted to nest by the water habitat. At migration time, parties of terns and waders may use the site as a temporary home while, in the winter months, there will be flocks of Pochard and Tufted Duck arriving from their northern and eastern breeding grounds. As with the tidal mudflats, this is a habitat that requires the spotting 'scope for, hidden among that distant raft of duck or feeding party of Coot, may be the occasional exciting bird that makes the day's outing worthwhile. Once again it must be stressed that entry into sites such as reservoirs and gravel pits is usually restricted and permission should be sought in advance.

FARMLAND

The term 'farmland' covers a wide range of areas from the extensive wheat fields with their autumn sparrow flocks to the small grazing pastures surrounded by dense hedges with the nesting Chaffinches and Greenfinches, and the deserted farm buildings where the Barn Owls and Stock Doves breed.

The birdwatcher must always respect the countryside but, in farmland, this is doubly important. Not only are the observations being made on private land, but it is land where thoughtless actions could seriously damage the farmer's livelihood.

At first glance, many farmland sites do not appear to be particularly exciting, but the more diverse the farming activity the more varied is the bird life that is likely to be encountered. Large expanses of a monoculture crop are unlikely to provide an interesting day's birdwatching, but a patchwork farmland with small copses, ponds and varied crops may be home for an exciting variety of birds. Because farmland covers such a high proportion of the British land area, the bird populations inhabiting it have been closely studied for many years and the importance of the hedgerows, uncultivated field corners, and ponds and ditches has been clearly demonstrated. Because of the extensive shooting and sporting interests of many land owners in the past, coverts and copses for the rearing of Pheasants and other gamebirds have been retained and are fully exploited by the wide range of other species to be found in these areas. As farming becomes more mechanized and intensified, the bird population will be restricted to less and less of the total farmland area and these retained copses and uncultivated areas will increase still further in their importance to bird life.

At all seasons of the year farmland is worth visiting. The bare ploughed fields of the autumn provide a feeding area for the migrant Lapwing flocks while, as winter approaches, the collections of thrushes descend upon the hedgerow berries and the numerous finches feed on the weed seeds at the field boundaries. In the height of winter the farm buildings provide shelter and the spilled animal feeds provide food during the coldest of weather while, with the coming of spring, every available nest site is exploited. The Pied Wagtail has taken over the space on top of the tractor engine, the Tree Sparrows are in the roof of the old barn while, in the distant hay meadow, a pair of Curlew are nesting and Tawny Owls are occupying the old pollarded willow.

GARDENS and TOWNS

Here the habitat needs no introduction to the birdwatcher. This is literally the back garden of the tens of thousands of active birdwatchers now living in Britain. Even the highly formalized and carefully tended gardens of the city parks hold bird life. These areas have been described as an oasis of green in a solid grey concrete desert. In these situations the birds have fully accepted man, for where else would the Jay and Wood Pigeon gather to feed on scraps thrown down by the passers' by, or the Starlings and Pied Wagtails collect nightly on the ledges of buildings or the plane trees among the street lights?

This is the habitat that all birdwatchers should know, but how many ignore its diversity and very high bird populations to rush off to some distant coastal site where exotic species may be encountered?

Birdwatching equipment and keeping records

Somewhere between the two extremes of a birdwatcher out for a quiet walk with a small pair of pocket binoculars and the eager birder searching for yet one more species to add to his or her list and weighed down by an assortment of optical equipment ranging from telescope and binoculars to a camera and sundry lenses, is the happy average that most birdwatchers enjoy. The key word must be 'enjoy'. Birdwatching for most people is a hobby; it is done for pleasure, relaxation, and enjoyment. Just how much you choose to spend and how much equipment you feel you need is entirely up to the individual – but the moment you stop enjoying birdwatching, you will stop taking part.

James Fisher in his excellent book, *Watching Birds*, opened his chapter on 'The tools of birdwatching' with the following rather tongue-in-cheek paragraph:

The birdwatcher has to use the following general tools for his job: a library, a note system, optical instruments for viewing (field glasses, telescope, etc) and for recording (camera). At one time he often combines two of these general instruments. Besides these he may have occasion to use more specialised instruments for specialised work. These may include traps, rings, stuffed and dead birds, dummy eggs, nestboxes, paint, mirrors, golf-balls, little cakes, tin plates, string, climbing irons, boats, motor-cycles, balloons, kites, aeroplanes, money, guns, and butter.

Behind this rather amusing list is a message – if you want to you can take birdwatching to almost any lengths. For most people, however, the enjoyment is something for the weekend and evenings, a spare-time occupation that takes them out into the fresh air to watch some of the most interesting wildlife in splendid surroundings. Birds have the advantage that they can be easily seen, they are colourful, they are active, and they are to be found everywhere. They are the ideal subjects for study as a part-time hobby.

The basic equipment needed for birdwatching is limited. For the purposes of this book, we shall only look at binoculars, telescopes, cameras, clothing, and record keeping. Each could become a major topic on its own, but perhaps you should only need

to seek further advice for photography which can be a more technical operation.

Binoculars

Today there are many different types of binoculars available in all shapes and sizes and from many different countries. Beware of gimmickry such as zoom binoculars, the combined binoculars and cameras, and binoculars with electronic focusing. A basic pair of prismatic binoculars is best. All binoculars are categorized by two numbers; for example, 9 × 40 or 10 × 50. The first figure refers to the magnification and the second to the diameter of the objective lens (the lens nearest to the object being viewed) measured in millimetres. The diameter of this lens gives an approximate indication of the amount of light that enters the binoculars. The larger the magnification the more light is required to make the binoculars useable. As a general guide, magnifications of 8 times, 9 times, or 10 times are very suitable for birdwatching and, again as a general rule, the larger the object lens the better, although they also become heavier. When it comes to the final choice, however, only trying the instrument under field conditions will tell you just which model is right for your own use. Try the weight; imagine that they are hanging round your neck all day. Are they too heavy? Are they comfortable to hold? Do they fit your eyes or pinch your nose? Can you easily adjust the focus?

Then, of course, there is the optical quality, but first the focusing must be set. Each pair of binoculars should have an adjustable eyepiece, usually the right-hand one. Close your right eye and focus the binoculars on a reasonably distant object with the central wheel using the left eye only. Then close the left eye and focus the right-hand side on the same object, using the adjustable eyepiece only. You have now set the binoculars for a field trial. If you are thinking of buying, there is one final piece of advice. Prices vary considerably from dealer to dealer, so check the magazines and price-lists for the best offers.

Telescopes

If binoculars are essential for birdwatching, then a telescope is a luxury that can add an extra dimension to the hobby, but is not vital. Many people ask if they should obtain a telescope and a good reply is, 'You will know when you are ready to carry a telescope all day'. The best instrument is a small lightweight prismatic spotting 'scope mounted on a lightweight, but firm tripod. When you have been birdwatching for some time and you have seen various 'scopes in use, you should have a good idea of what is required. More and more models are becoming available and it is almost as difficult to decide on a telescope as it is to select binoculars. Do not be in a rush to obtain a telescope; bide your time and try them out. Most birdwatchers will be only too pleased to let you try their own 'scopes and discuss their merits and faults. Very high power in a telescope is not necessarily a good idea for the larger the magnification the greater the problem with light gathering, heat haze, shaking in the wind, and so on. A useful magnification is times 20 or times 25 with a 60 millimetre object lens although, unlike binoculars, zoom telescopes have their uses. Again, field trials are a must to ensure that you obtain the telescope that is most suitable for your own use but, whatever you choose, you must be able to hold it quite still. You will need a good quality tripod, car door clamp, or shoulder butt to hold the instrument steady.

Cameras

Bird photography is a specialized art requiring skills and equipment beyond the scope of this book. If you want to find out more about it you should refer to one or more of the books mentioned in the Further Reading List.

The general birdwatcher may sometimes get the chance to take good photographs of birds with a 35 millimetre camera and telephoto lens, but you should seek expert advice before you invest the quite considerable sum of money required to purchase the necessary equipment.

The Association of British Natural History Photographic Societies has produced a code of conduct which is published on their behalf by the Royal Society for the Protection of Birds. Intending bird photographers should consult this code, which is too detailed to reproduce in full here. It begins with a very important statement: 'The welfare of the subject is more important than the photograph'. It is probably worth bearing in mind that the truly dedicated bird photographer almost ceases to be a birdwatcher in the usual sense because this particular branch of the hobby becomes all-absorbing.

Clothing

The key must be comfort and subdued colours. Luminous orange anoraks, bright blue wellingtons, and vivid yellow hats are out, and browns, greys, and greens are in! Under normal circumstances, slacks or jeans, a sweater, and a lightweight anorak should suffice together with sweaters or a quilted anorak on cold or windy days, and a set of waterproof trousers and a jacket for the wet days. Birdwatching in the rain is never much fun, birds tend to be quiet and hidden, and it is difficult to use binoculars. On the other hand, if you are out for the day in Britain, it is quite likely to rain so it makes sense to carry lightweight waterproofs in a day pack as well as food and drink.

Footwear is very important, too, and wet or cold feet always seem much more uncomfortable than other parts of the anatomy. If it is wet or likely to be wet underfoot then wellington boots are a must; in dry conditions walking boots or stout shoes are invaluable depending upon the terrain. That day pack also comes in handy for carrying an extra pair of socks. The unimaginable joy and pleasure of changing from wet socks to dry socks has to be experienced to be believed – and how envious your companions are!

A typical page from a birdwatcher's notebook. But remember that the kind of notes you take and the records you keep are up to you. Above all you should enjoy your hobby.

Record keeping

You must decide for yourself whether or not to keep detailed records of your observations. Remember that birdwatching is a hobby and is meant to be fun – if you find it a chore to take copious notes then you will soon give up birdwatching so, once again, perhaps a compromise can be reached.

One possibility is simply to keep a list of the species seen, be it daily, yearly, or over the recorder's lifetime. A detailed diary with very explicit notes, and fully indexed, is another alternative. Record cards filed under the name of the species or the location leaves room for growth, as does a loose-leaf record book(s).

Keeping notes is a very personal pastime but, ideally, you should have a note book in your pocket at all times. This is not just to record the birds that you see but, as birdwatching becomes more and more of a way of life rather than just a spare-time occupation, you will find that you wish to note so many different things. One of the author's field notebooks, for example, contains details of a Honey Buzzard *(Pernis apivrorus)* passage on the Adriatic coast together with how to say 'good morning' in Serbo–Croat, the description of an unidentified blue butterfly with a friend's name and address, the dates for a world conference on birds of prey together with the description of the flight action of an unidentified eagle.

The memory can be surprisingly untrustworthy and it is very useful to keep good field notes so that you can check the identity of a bird later or so that you can confirm any other facts.

Some birdwatching terms

adult a bird in its final plumage. Birds progress with a series of moults through a number of plumages, to adult plumage. This usually indicates maturity although a few species will breed in apparently immature plumage. Many species have different adult plumages in winter and summer.

auk the general term for a family of birds, the Alcidae which, in Britain, comprises the following breeding species: Guillemot, Razorbill, Puffin, and Black Guillemot.

avian relating to birds.

bird of prey a collective term referring to the day-flying predators, ie falcons, hawks, buzzards, eagles, etc. In general use, does not include the owls.

birding Americanism for birdwatching which has become popular in Britain and includes all activities from bird ringing to bird photography. Similarly, a birdwatcher has become known as a birder.

breck or breckland: a rather dry impoverished area of East Anglia, now largely reclaimed for agriculture or planted for forestry.

breeding cycle period that covers all activities relating to a species' breeding, from first establishment of territory and pair formation to the eventual independence of the final brood.

brood unfledged young of a pair before independence.

bunting general term for a family of birds, the Emberizidae, related to the finches, which, in Britain, includes the breeding species: Yellowhammer, Cirl Bunting, Reed Bunting, and Corn Bunting.

call birds' vocal noises that are not song, including flight calls, alarm notes etc. (*See* song.)

canopy topmost branches in a woodland. Usually refers to the summer season when leaves cut out sunlight creating a 'closed canopy' with no light in dense woodland and an 'open canopy' with light reaching the woodland floor where trees are sparser.

clutch the number of eggs laid in a nest by one female.

colony the collection of several pairs of the same species for nesting.

communal where several individuals, usually of the same species, gather together for the same activity, such as feeding or roosting.

coppice a woodland management practice where trees, often chestnut or hazel, are cut at ground level every 7-15 years.

cosmopolitan occurrence in a wide range of habitats and/or of wide geographical distribution.

covey flock of game birds which may comprise one or more families.

creche collection of unfledged young from more than one brood.

crepuscular active in the half-light of dawn and dusk.

cryptic coloration coloured to blend with the background and thus be difficult to see.

dabbling duck duck that obtains it food by up-ending or by sifting water through its bill in the shallows. (*See* diving duck.)

dispersal random movement of all or part of a bird population. Usually refers to the young after independence.

display behaviour by birds in response to certain conditions. It often involves exaggerated movements and is most closely connected with breeding, but other displays take place in defence of territory, for aggression at a food supply, etc.

diurnal active during daylight. (*See* nocturnal.)

diver general term for a family of birds, the Gaviidae, which includes the Red-throated Diver, but also used to indicate any species which dives to obtain its food.

diving duck duck that obtains its food by diving beneath the surface. (*See* dabbling duck.)

falcon general term for a family of birds, the Falconidae, swift-flying birds of prey which, in Britain, includes breeding species: Kestrel, Merlin, Hobby, and Peregrine.

fen wetland habitat which generally includes dense vegetation and scrub that has developed as open water has become overgrown.

feral species that were once domesticated or held in captivity but which have now developed wild living populations.

fledge the point at which young birds leave the nest or gain the power of flight.

game bird collective name used for grouse and pheasants, but legally the expression 'game' has a wider meaning.

gape inside of a bird's bill or, sometimes, the soft fleshy area visible at the base of the bill, particularly in young birds.

habitat type of area that a particular species lives in.

hybrid result of cross-breeding between two different species.

immature bird not in full adult plumage.

indigenous native to the area; not a casual or introduced species.

'jizz' the overall appearance and impression of a bird. Difficult to define but includes movement and behaviour as well as physical appearance.

juvenile a bird in its first plumage, rarely retained many weeks after fledging.

lek display ground where males congregate and indulge in a communal display. Most commonly Black Grouse and Ruff.

mandible one half of a bird's bill, hence upper and lower mandibles.

migrant bird moving from one geographical area to another; a summer migrant is in Britain for the summer, the winter migrant in the winter, and a passage migrant only passes through.

migration the movement of a population from one area to another.

mobbing where one, or a collection of several individuals/species react with agitation or aggression to an intruder. Small birds frequently mob birds of prey, owls, or cats, and humans may be mobbed if the nests are approached too closely.

moult changing plumage, usually at least annually, when old feathers are shed and new feathers grow to replace them.

nocturnal active at night. (*See* diurnal.)

ornithology the study of birds.

pair bond the result of often highly stylized and ritualized behaviour which enables two birds to remain together either for a season, or for life.

passage journey of a migrant. A bird on passage is usually at a point between its summering and wintering grounds.

pellet the regurgitated indigestible portion of a bird's meal, usually from birds of prey and owls.

plumage feathered covering of a bird, usually referred to by season or age, thus winter plumage or immature plumage.

pollard a woodland management practice where trees, often willows, are cut at a height of a few metres above the ground at intervals of several years.

predator usually describing birds of prey and owls, but more widely to include any species which kills another for food.

race geographical form of a species which has developed small but consistent differences, not always immediately apparent, as a result of breeding in isolation from other members of the same species. (*See* subspecies.)

range the geographical area over which the species occurs.

rarity uncommon species, but degrees of rarity can vary and a vagrant (*viz*) is generally considered the rarest of all.

resident permanently in one area.

ring a light band, inscribed with an address and number that can be placed around a bird's leg to help study migration and other aspects of a bird's life history. Colour rings can be used to identify individuals without having to trap them.

roost where birds spend the night, or other resting period such as during a high tide.

saltings coastal green marsh, open to the tides and usually covered on the higher tides, but often left exposed.

seabird usually species that spend at least some of their lives over the open sea rather than just beside it.

sedentary not migratory.

skulking keeping hidden in the vegetation, difficult to observe.

song generally the more musical aspects of a bird's voice, rather than the call (*viz*). Mechanical 'song' occurs in the form of drumming from woodpeckers and snipe.

'standing ground' specifically refers to Herons, where the birds not attending the nest during the early part of the breeding cycle spend the day standing.

subadult a bird not quite in full adult plumage, but having lost most of the signs of immaturity.

subspecies *See* race.

summer visitor an individual/species that arrives for the summer months only. (*See* winter visitor.)

summering usually individuals that remain

territory usually an area of land that a bird will defend for nesting purposes, but can be a feeding or wintering territory.

tundra any vast open stretches of land in Arctic regions, usually covered with low-growing vegetation such as mosses and lichens or stunted bushes.

vagrant an extreme rarity *(viz)*.

wader a collection of bird families which includes the plovers and sandpipers, and that are characterized by long legs and/or bills that are used in specialized feeding.

waterfowl birds of a wide variety of families that spend a proportion of their time on water. Includes all wildfowl *(viz)*.

wildfowl a family of birds, the Anatidae, which comprises the ducks, geese, and swans.

winter visitor an individual/species that arrives for the winter months oinly. (*See* summer visitor.)

wintering usually individuals that remain during the winter when the majority of the species have departed for the normal wintering grounds. (*See* summering.)

A calendar of birds

JANUARY

The weather is dull and grey and a bitter cold wind sweeps in off the sea across the shallow waters of the estuary. Behind the sea wall a bare field is starting to show the first signs of the sprouting winter wheat, while at one end a solid grey block becomes slightly restless as the individual Knots in the tightly packed flock that has sat out the high tide begin to realize that their enforced spell of inactivity is nearly over. They are anxious to begin feeding, for the cold winter weather demands a high food intake to maintain body warmth. On a nearby island in a gravel pit the packed Oystercatchers have similarly sat out the tide and they too are becoming restless and starting their continual piping calls. Everywhere the scene is similar – returning activity. The Turnstones and Sanderlings have sat near the water's edge on a quiet length of beach, the Brent Geese have ridden out the choppy waters on the sheltered side of the estuary, sleeping and preening away the hours until their staple diet, the eelgrass, is revealed on the mud as the tide falls. At last, the waters begin to retreat, dropping back against the wind which seems determined to keep the mud covered until the last possible moment. The birds can return to feed and exploit the rich animal life left stranded by the retreating water or hidden in the thick rich mud that has accumulated over the years as the river-bed deposits have met the sea in a vast delta, now largely harnessed and controlled by man. The first activity comes from the waders that have spent the high tide beside the water's edge but, as the area of exposed mud continues to grow, vast clouds of birds leave the fields and gravel islands to sweep across the tide line and settle on the mud. There is no delay, no ceremony, the birds begin to feed as soon as they land for, within a few short hours, they must obtain enough food to carry them through the next high tide period. The more mud that becomes exposed, the larger the birds that begin to move. Following the Knots and Redshanks, the Oystercatchers leave the islands, until finally, from some distant field, the distinctive calls of the Curlew herald the last and biggest of the waders and their flocks come tumbling from the sky.

Red-throated Diver   *Gavia stellata*

The smart, colourful plumage of the breeding season has been lost and the breeding lochs of Scotland deserted. At the height of the winter the divers have become strictly marine although an unexpected severe gale blowing in from the Atlantic or battering the North Sea coast will occasionally deposit rather weak, often lightly oiled individuals at inland reservoirs or gravel pits where they look rather out of place among the more familiar ducks and grebes. The drab grey and white of winter plumage seems well in keeping with a cold, blustery January day at almost any British coastal site. They may be seen flying past a headland either singly or in small groups showing their distinctive hump-backed silhouette. Or they may be found in some sheltered bay regularly diving for food, but behaving as individuals and not mingling with the parties of sea ducks and grebes that may be sharing the site. In common with so many of our wintering seabirds, the divers are, unfortunately, highly susceptible to marine oil pollution, and a search of the tide-line, particularly following a period of gales, will often reveal corpses of a variety of species, mainly auks, but including a small selection of divers.

55cm

Gadwall   *Anas strepera*

This is a rather insignificant-looking duck, easily overlooked among the mass of wintering wildfowl on some favoured freshwater pool or marsh. Rather restricted as a breeding species, by January the numbers have been swelled by Continental immigrants but, with a total British wintering population of only about 1500 birds, it is not one of the commonest dabbling ducks. In general, the Gadwall looks rather like a female Mallard, but, unlike the Mallard, it will rarely become tame or associate with man, and it presents an altogether sleeker, greyer appearance. In flight the square white speculum on the trailing edge of the wing is diagnostic. Virtually all the British breeding population, apart perhaps for some birds in Scotland, has resulted from introduced or escaped birds. Their stronghold is in East Anglia where the largest concentrations of wintering individuals are to be found. A January count of 2 to 300 birds on flooded meadows, broads, or gravel pits in this area is not unusual. In addition to looking for the Gadwall among the other winter duck flocks, look closely at feeding concentrations of Coot *(Fulica atra)*, because the two species have now established a regular winter feeding association. A regularly diving Coot will have one or two Gadwall in close attendance waiting eagerly for the feeding bird to reappear from its dive. No sooner does the Coot break the surface than the Gadwall are by its side and, as well as feeding on any food items in the disturbed water, they will readily steal weed.

50cm

Scaup

Aythya marila

January birdwatchers on the coast of Scotland or on the shores of the Irish Sea are most likely to encounter the wintering flocks of this northern duck. Arctic Siberia and Iceland are the breeding areas for the birds that appear in British waters, although their numbers are low compared with the population elsewhere in north-west Europe; Denmark, for example, supports some 50 000 wintering Scaup. The largest concentrations in Britain are to be found in the Seafield/Leith area of the Firth of Forth (OS map 66) where counts of over 20 000 have been recorded although numbers are now regularly less than 10 000. This marked winter concentration is the result of a sewage outfall where waste grain is discharged from nearby distilleries. As pollution control improves Scaup will become more dependent upon their natural diet of marine shellfish. In the long term, this will probably benefit the species because such an artificial concentration is highly susceptible to a serious pollution incident. Away from the northern areas, Scaup may be seen in midwinter in small numbers at almost any coastal site, occasionally moving on to freshwater pools just inland, where they can hide themselves away among the local Tufted Duck (*Aythya fuligula*).

48cm

White-fronted Goose

Anser albifrons

Goose-watching is fun and exciting, very much a winter occupation, but at times very frustrating. Geese are wary birds and will not usually allow close approach. Most views are obtained as they noisily change their feeding grounds, or flight out on to the exposed mud of the estuary as the tide falls. Patience and the aid of a good telescope will provide some exciting views, for the sounds, the places, and the birds that the goose-watcher will encounter all have a romanticism of their own. The goose-hunting winter birdwatcher has one great advantage because geese have traditional sites to which they return year after year. During migration or in very severe winters, some individuals may appear, often in mixed flocks, at very unlikely sites, but a normal winter will find the geese back at the regular estuary or coastal marsh. The White-fronted Goose is very much a bird of the south and west, with the largest numbers of the Russian breeding birds at the now very famous Wildfowl Trust site at Slimbridge, Gloucestershire (OS map 172). The White-fronted Geese that bred in Greenland differ from the Russian birds by being darker and having longer, orange (rather than pink) bills. The entire population of this Greenland group numbers some 12 000 individuals, all of of which winter in the British Isles, principally in Ireland where approximately half of the world's population is to be found at the Wexford Slobs. Elsewhere, the goose-hunter will find about 4000 Greenland White-fronts on Islay (OS map 60).

70cm

Bean Goose

Anser fabalis

This is the scarcest member of the group that a goose-hunter can expect to encounter in Britain each winter. Formerly much commoner and quite widespread, now there are probably less than 200 Bean Geese at only two regular wintering sites in Britain, although cold weather on the Continent may well result in displaced birds appearing at almost any coastal locality from Kent to Scotland. The better known of the two sites is at Buckenham Fen in Norfolk (OS map 134) where an observation hide has been provided to enable views of the birds to be obtained without disturbing the flock. The second site is in the valley of the river Dee in Scotland (OS map 83).

75cm

Brent Goose

Branta bernicla

Almost every estuary and harbour in south-east England in January will hold a sizeable population of Brent Geese, and this attractive bird, the smallest of our wintering geese, is one of the earliest to arrive and easiest to see. There has been a dramatic increase in the numbers of this delightful goose and its nature has become more confiding since it was removed from the list of legitimate quarry for the wildfowler. This action was taken because of a serious decline in the population of the bird throughout its range following the loss of its staple food, eel-grass, from disease. Sitting on the sea wall which separates the Hampshire and Isle of Wight Naturalists' Trust reserve at Farlington Marshes from the RSPB's reserve at Langstone Harbour (OS maps 196; 197) our goose-watcher can spend a splendid, if perhaps somewhat cold, January day enjoying the wealth of bird life that should include as many as 5000 of the dark-bellied Brent Geese, several of which now exploit the grazing on nearby meadows and crops as the recovering eelgrass supplies are exhausted by the increasing goose population. These dark-bellied Brents originate from Arctic Siberia and may be found in substantial flocks around the south-east coast from the Solent to the Wash. The very closely related pale-bellied Brent Goose originates from Arctic breeding grounds in Canada and Greenland but Ireland provides the only wintering site for this race in the whole of Europe. The largest concentrations are to be found at Strangford Lough, County Down; and Tralee and Dingle Bays, County Kerry. Our January goose-hunter may wish to make just one more journey in search of a rather special Brent Goose population. Each winter, on the Northumberland coast near Holy Island (OS map 75) a few hundred pale-bellied Brent Geese from Spitsbergen and Franz Josef Land are to be found. These are part of January's most northerly Brent Goose population.

60cm

Ptarmigan

Lagopus mutus

The Highlands of Scotland attract the summer birdwatcher but rarely receive attention in the winter months when lack of ornithological variety and inclement weather are not conducive to good birding. Some species, however, remain in this far-from-attractive climate and, in January, above 760 metres among the rocky terrain and winter snow, the Ptarmigan has acquired its all-white winter plumage. Only the tail remains dark to contrast with the otherwise ideal camouflage. Well equipped with strong, feathered legs and feet, this least familiar member of the grouse family will dig in the snow to obtain its food of shoots and buds. If the winter weather becomes too severe for even this hardy bird, the Ptarmigan moves to some of the lower crags and sheltered valley bottoms. Generally, however, the Ptarmigan rarely occurs in areas that man regularly frequents, although the increasing use of the Scottish Highlands for winter sports activities may well change this and birdwatchers may be able to observe the bird in summer and winter relatively easily.

36 cm

Water Rail

Rallus aquaticus

This secretive bird of reed beds and marshes is structurally very thin to enable it to move among the dense vegetation with the minimum of disturbance to disclose its presence. Indeed, the entire bird seems to have been compressed laterally. It rarely flies, preferring to esape by running on its very long toes that are specially adapted to enable it to walk across soft mud and floating vegetation. The Water Rail's presence in a particular locality is usually confirmed by the distinctive loud squealing call originating from the dense waterside vegetation. The Water Rail is very difficult to observe but a frosty January day, with a thin layer of ice on the water and the reed bed frozen at the base, will force the Rails into the open in search of sites with running water or other unfrozen patches. At such times they can be extremely tame providing the unobtrusive observer with some excellent views of an otherwise mysterious bird. At these times it often becomes clear that this is not necessarily a bird of pleasant habits for, although the normal diet is varied and includes insects, worms, fishes, seeds, and berries, observations during cold weather periods have added some surprising additions to the list. Small birds and mammals attracted to the same unfrozen sites are killed or stunned by a sharp blow on the back of the head and then eaten. Apart from in northern and western Scotland, this species may be encountered by any January birdwatcher who frequents marshes and wet areas with dense vegetation, but the Water Rail is more likely to be found in the south and east of the country where the winter population is swelled by Continental immigrants. Try visiting the National Nature Reserve at Stodmarsh in Kent (OS map 179) or any of the reserves on the north Norfolk coast (OS maps 132; 133).

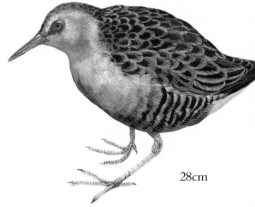

28cm

Oystercatcher
Haematopus ostralegus

This is probably the noisiest of the winter waders that flock to the estuaries and coastal mud flats throughout the country. The striking black-and-white plumage and large, brilliant-red bill make this an easy bird to identify, unlike the massed flocks of the smaller grey and brown waders. It is unfortunately named for, although our Oystercatcher's diet includes a wide range of marine molluscs, such as cockles and limpets, oysters are very rarely eaten. Experiments in captivity, however, have shown that the bird is quite capable of opening small oysters successfully. In recent years the Oystercatcher has been spreading inland as a breeding species, following river valleys and colonizing farmland and gravel pits until it now nests throughout Scotland and northern England, and even central southern England has a small breeding population. By January, however, the entire population is back to the coast and the species has become extremely rare inland. The total wintering population in Britain is about 200 000 birds with our winter ornithologists encountering the largest concentrations on four estuaries: on the east coast at the Wash (OS map 131); in Wales on the Burry (OS map 159); and in the north-west at Morecambe Bay (OS map 97) and the Solway (OS maps 84; 85).

43cm

Knot
Calidris canutus

At three RSPB reserves at the Wash, Snettisham (OS map 132), the Dee estuary, Gayton Sands (OS map 117), and Morecambe Bay (OS map 97), you can expect an ornithological spectacle of immense proportions. You must time your visit to take account of the tides. Indeed, if you plan to watch birds at the coast in winter, a tide-table is invaluable. You should arrive at the site and position yourself about three hours before the full high tide is expected. Forced off their feeding grounds by the steadily rising water, the birds bunch and accumulate, gathering into dense concentrations as the available mud is steadily reduced. The different species of waders segregate themselves but, most numerous are the Knot, looking grey and uniform. As the tens of thousands take to the air and wheel en masse over the incoming tide they look like a controlled bank of smoke or distant cloud, rising and falling in unique evolutions. Gaining height, and with each flock of many thousands combining to form an even larger aerial throng of grey, they make for the chosen high-tide roost: perhaps a ploughed field behind the sea wall or an exposed sandbank not to be covered by that particular tide. At Snettisham they may congregate on the specially constructed shingle islands in the gravel pits that are overlooked by the reserve's observation hides. But whichever site they choose and wherever they settle, it is immediately transformed into a solid carpet of grey, and there the birds remain until the falling tide again allows them to feed.

25cm

Great Black-backed Gull
Larus marinus

As its scientific name suggests, this is the most coastal or marine of all the gulls. Small numbers can be encountered inland at winter roosts or at feeding sites on rubbish tips or even farmland. The species is always in a minority, however, although it stands head and shoulders above the smaller more familiar Black-headed Gulls *(L. ridibundus)*. Strong winds and January storms will swell the numbers in the harbours and sheltered bays as those individuals feeding well out to sea seek temporary respite. They will follow large or small boats gliding slowly with their heads perpetually turning and searching for discarded scraps or food items that may be made available in the boat's wake. Close inshore the tide-line provides a wealth of winter food. Stranded whales and fishes, the corpses of oiled seabirds, or food items stolen from the smaller, less pugnacious gulls, are all readily attacked and eaten. With its large, heavy bill and thick, strong neck the Great Black-back can dismember a corpse as easily as the most efficient raptor. In cold January weather, when many small birds are forced to undertake weather migrations, fleeing the approaching snow or freezing temperatures, the Great Black-backed Gulls make short work of any weak or undernourished bird attempting to cross a coastal stretch of water. Thrushes or larks struggling to keep airborne will be buffeted into the water, seized, and even swallowed whole.

70cm

Long-eared Owl
Asio otus

A particularly nocturnal owl, the Long-eared Owl is probably one of the least known, for it is rarely associated with man and lacks a distinctive voice. From mid-January, however, on crisp clear nights, the Long-eared Owls start calling even though many individuals are still in communal roosts. These are probably the Continental immigrants waiting to return to the European mainland of Scandinavia where spring is much later in arriving. The undramatic 'oo-oo-oo . . .' of the song does not carry far among the dense conifer plantations that the species prefers, but, if the night-wandering ornithologist is tuned for the sound, the song, plus perhaps the occasional wing clap as the bird circles a clearing, point to the species' presence. A daytime roost of several individuals in a thick hawthorn clump is often exposed by the collection of droppings and pellets of undigested prey items on the ground beneath, both signs of regular usage for the site. If you approach the clump stealthily in daylight and carefully scan the branches you may have splendid views of the birds as they 'freeze' into a stance which the passerby would normally overlook. At these times the bird exhibits its ability to appear in two completely contrasting shapes – tall and thin with ear-tufts erect, or short and round with ear-tufts invisible.

36cm

Shore Lark
Eremophila alpestris

Shore Lark is a most appropriate name for this species in January, but it is far from applicable outside the British winter. It is a widespread species occurring throughout most of Europe and Asia, living in the higher and more northern habitats, as well as in North America where it is found in a far wider selection of sites. It would perhaps be better known by its American name of 'Horned Lark' after the black horn-like feathering on the crown. In the winter months, however, Scandinavian breeding birds leave the tundra and mountain tops and small numbers regularly arrive to spend the winter on the beaches of eastern England from Yorkshire south to Kent. At this time they become true 'shore' larks because they are rarely found away from the beach, feeding on the tide-line and saltings, often in mixed flocks with those other winter visitors to the coast, the Snow and Lapland Buntings *(Plectrophenax nivalis* and *Calcarius lapponicus).* Single birds will attach themselves to parties of Skylarks *(Alauda arvensis),* but small groups or flocks will remain independent and they are often difficult to see as they crouch among the sparse coastal vegetation which provides the winter food source. The north Norfolk coast, particularly Salthouse (OS map 133) is one of several of the more regular wintering localities, but each of the east-coast counties has their favourite spots.

16·5cm

Raven
Corvus corax

Formerly a scavenger of London streets, the Raven has come into conflict with man and is now confined to the remoter areas of Wales, Scotland, and Ireland, with a smaller population in the north and south-west of England. It is the nearest substitute that Britain can find for a vulture. The bird is forever in search of suitable food and anything will be quickly attacked with the massive, powerful bill. Occasionally, large numbers of Ravens will assemble at food sources; flocks on Welsh rubbish tips are regular and there is a quite amazing record of 800 congregating to feed on stranded whales in the Shetlands. This is one of the earliest breeding species in Britain, with the majority of pairs sitting on their completed clutches by mid-February. As a result, considerable activity on the breeding grounds and around the nest sites takes place in January, often in the severest of weather. There can be few birds which have the birdwatcher concerned with the breeding scene on a cold January morning, but the display flighting of a pair of Ravens is truly spectacular and even includes rolls, upside-down flight, and somersaults. Surely one of the most dramatic aspects of this display is the rapid loss of height on closed wings when the bird will drop from a considerable altitude only to swing upwards again with its own momentum. The air currents around the rocky sea cliffs and inland crags all aid the birds in this most spectacular of manoeuvres.

63cm

Wren

Troglodytes troglodytes

This familiar little bird with the upturned tail is likely to attract January attention only if the weather is either of two extremes. An unusually mild month with no hint of cold can induce the birds to sing – and one cannot fail to be amazed at the sheer volume of noise originating from such a tiny throat. Authors in the past have produced a wide range of adjectives to describe this outpouring including 'vehement', 'intimidatory', 'rallying', 'ebullient', 'shattering', 'staccato', and so on. In full voice and on a calm, clear day in January the Wren's song will carry for as much as 800 metres. In complete contrast, a severely cold, freezing January will be detrimental to the Wren population and birds will not sing. Persistent frosts, which freeze the hedge bottoms and sheltered patches where the species normally seeks its food, are the most destructive. It is possible for a population to make a dramatic recovery, however; the estimated million or so breeding pairs in Britain after the cold winter of 1963-64 had increased to some ten million pairs only ten years later. One immediate response to a freezing January is a marked increase in communal roosting. As the temperature drops lower and lower, Wrens gather together to help one another keep warm, and surprising numbers can squeeze into a small space. Among the many observations are ten in a coconut shell, nine in an old Song Thrush's nest, and the quite remarkable totals of forty-six, fifty-one, and sixty-one in nest boxes. One of these even managed to feature on a regional television programme.

9·5 cm

Chiffchaff

Phylloscopus collybita

Small warblers are principally part of the summer birdwatchers' scene in Britain. Only two species, Dartford and Cetti's Warblers *(Sylvia undata* and *Cettia cetti)*, are looked upon as true residents which are likely to be encountered throughout the year. The Chiffchaff, however, is mainly a summer visitor but it is not one of those species that departs each autumn for wintering grounds south of the Sahara, and many remain in the Mediterranean basin. Chiffchaffs are never completely absent from Britain and the further south and west you travel in January the more warblers you are likely to discover. A mid-winter visitor to the Isles of Scilly (OS map 203) will almost certainly locate a few because a wintering population of twenty or so birds is not unusual. A fine, sunny day will start the birds singing and, although the familiar 'chiff-chaff' call is to be expected, a rather sweet warbling subsong is sometimes heard and you should be careful not to mistake a Chiffchaff for a Willow Warbler *(P. trochilus)*. The relatively large numbers of wintering Chiffchaffs in southern England make the recording of the first spring arrivals extremely difficult and Chiffchaffs are now reported in many countries throughout the year. It is one of the first species to disappear, however, if January weather is severe.

11cm

Blackcap

Sylvia atricapilla

The Blackcap is another warbler that our winter birdwatcher can expect to locate because, once again, a small but regular population remains in Britain throughout the colder months of the year. Unlike the Chiffchaff, this species can be encountered regularly much further north, with January records in some years from the far north of Scotland. The largest numbers are always in the south and west, however, and there is a regular Irish wintering population. Because of the lack of winter birdwatchers here, the picture is incomplete. Many people now feed birds in winter, and more and more Blackcaps have been recorded exploiting this new food source. It has long been known that these wintering Blackcaps are great opportunist feeders and eat a wide range of berries and fruits, but bird tables are now regularly playing winter hosts. During the winter, these insect-eating summer residents are now discovering bread, and hang, like tits, on the fat and kitchen scraps. Indeed, in several areas Blackcaps dominate the bird table and chase away the more usual Robins and Chaffinches *(Erithacus rubicula* and *Fringilla coelebs)*. The majority of the wintering individuals are males, distinguished by their black caps, but even some of the 'females' (which have brown caps) may be immature males. All juvenile Blackcaps leave the nest with brown caps but, during the autumn, a moult of the plumage changes the head feathers – the males become black and the females remain brown. However, a proportion of these young males retain a varying amount of brown tipping to the black feathers and the crown can look brown. The normal pattern is for the males of migrant birds to arrive back on their breeding grounds shortly in advance of the females, so it is not surprising that the majority of the most northerly Blackcaps in January should be male.

14cm

Siskin

Carduelis spinus

A riverside stroll in January, where the banks are lined with alders and willows, will often reveal a mixed flock of small finches feeding in a similar manner to the familiar tits that hang from the bags of peanuts in the garden. Suspended on the outer twigs of the trees, hanging upside-down, continually on the move, and twittering quietly but perpetually, are the mixed groups of Siskins and Redpolls *(C. flammea)*. Outside Scotland and Ireland, the Siskin is a rather scarce breeding bird but, in the winter months, Continental immigrants swell the population and the bird becomes a feature of several lowland areas. A rather shrill, drawn-out flight call is usually the first indication that the species is in the area but, when viewed feeding, the greenish-yellow appearance with yellow flashes in the rather short, forked tail, prominent yellow wing bar, and black on crown and chin in the male are all distinctive.

12cm

FEBRUARY

A light covering of snow has disappeared in the midday sun, but several nights of hard frost have left the surface of the fields hard and firm. Until recently, they have been thick and sticky with mud which clung to the soles of the rubber boots so that walking became more and more difficult as the boots became heavier and heavier. With the frosts the open fields can no longer provide feeding grounds, the Rooks cannot probe and thrust for the grubs and larvae, and the Lapwings, which normally peck delicately at the surface, have been deprived of food and have been forced to leave. They left in compact flocks travelling in a southerly or south-westerly direction, heading towards a milder climate and, if necessary, deserting British shores, but returning immediately the weather improves. The frost, however, has yet to reach the hedge bottoms or invade the environs of the farm buildings. The birds move in from the open fields seeking new feeding areas. Snipe can be flushed from beneath the hawthorn bushes, their normal ditches now covered by a thin sheet of ice. In these situations they form a rare feeding association with the Pheasants which, under these circumstances, are reluctant to leave the safety of the copses and woodland edge although small numbers penetrate the hedgerow bottoms. The finch flocks have withdrawn from the open fields, seeking a new food source that is not frozen to the ground and finding it around the feeding troughs and stock pens where spilled animal food and water are available daily during the coldest of weather. The familiar farmyard sparrows and Chaffinches are joined by the less familiar Yellowhammers and Reed Buntings, species not normally found in close association with man. The Pied Wagtails, which will eventually nest somewhere among the farm buildings, are tamer than ever, spending more time indoors than out. Suddenly the weather changes; after a week of cold, February has become mild and damp and lives up to its name of 'February fill-dyke'. Almost immediately, the change is apparent; the Fieldfares and Redwings lose their interest in the hawthorn berries and return to foraging on the grass meadow; the Lapwings are back and even start to show signs of their spring display; while the cock Pheasant is once more to be seen strutting across the open fields. And are we sure that there was a Yellowhammer around the barn?

Heron

Ardea cinerea

The first of the birds may have returned to the nesting colony in December but their numbers build up slowly during January, with most of the older, more established breeding pairs present at the old nests by the beginning of February. The young, first-time breeding birds will not arrive until later in the month or even late March. Early February is occupied with re-establishing the pair bond and rebuilding the previous season's nest. The birds are highly vocal, often displaying with elaborate bowing and wing-spreading movements, and large numbers of sticks are carried to the nests although these are often stolen if a nest is left unguarded. At this time, Herons have bright-pink bills which form an important part of the breeding display. With the arrival of the first eggs, usually in the third week of the month, the bills return to a less striking yellow coloration although they can become pink again if the eggs are lost and the parents need to restart the breeding cycle. February is an important month for the 'standing ground', an area close by the heronry where the off-duty birds, usually the males, stand motionless as part of the highly ritualized breeding behaviour. These areas are often excellent places at which to watch Herons. The total British breeding population is about 6000 pairs and two of the largest heronries in Britain are to be found in the south-east at the RSPB's reserve in Northward Hill, Kent (OS map 178) and at Walthamstow reservoirs, Essex (OS map 177).

90cm

Wigeon

Anas penelope

Although the Wigeon is a breeding duck in northern Britain, the population is swollen during the winter with birds from Iceland and Russian Siberia. This substantial wintering population can increase as a result of influxes following cold continental weather in February. At its peak the number of birds can be more than 200 000. The Wigeon is mainly a coastal bird feeding on the eelgrass at low tide and grazing on the saltmarsh when the mud is covered. It may also be found at inland sites where it favours flooded grass meadows and feeds on the short, close-cropped grass. The principal inland site for Wigeon is certainly the reserves of the RSPB, Cambridgeshire Naturalists' Trust, and Wildfowl Trust at the Ouse Washes (OS map 143). Here it is possible to see as many as 35 000 individuals at a time when Britain is playing host to some 50 per cent of the north-west European population. For coastal sites, the Highland regions of Scotland hold several thousands of birds in the Firth of Moray (OS map 27); Cromarty (OS maps 21 and 26); and Dornoch (OS map 21).

45cm

Pink-footed Goose   *Anser brachyrhynchus*

In the middle of February, the Pink-footed Goose is well established on the British wintering grounds, with the largest numbers on the east coast of Scotland. One of the traditional goose-watching sites is at Aberlady Bay (OS map 66) where the regular dawn and dusk flighting provides a magnificent spectacle. Far out on the tidal mud the birds feel safe and secure, free from disturbance or attack by predator. As dusk approaches and, if the tide is out, the skeins of high-flying geese appear from inland, deserting the agricultural land on which they have been feeding for much of the day. In noisy groups the geese fly on as if about to fly out into the Firth itself when suddenly, in tumbling, twisting parties, they drop from the sky to settle on the vast expanse of mud. More and more birds with their continual 'wink-wink' calls, arrive at the site, the pale-grey forewing catching the evening light as the Geese touch down to swell the numbers of the distant grey mass accumulating far from shore. Although Scotland is definitely the winter home of this species in Britain, the English birdwatcher can at least witness something of the spectacle by watching the movements that take place each year on the mud flats of The Wash (OS maps 131 and 132).

70cm

Barnacle Goose   *Branta leucopsis*

Although it is occasionally seen in summer, when small numbers of feral or escaped birds may appear at any site and even nest and rear young, this is a winter goose with traditional sites which rarely vary. Three different breeding populations have three different wintering grounds and all affect Britain to a greater or lesser extent. The breeding birds in Greenland travel via an Icelandic stepping stone to the wintering grounds of western Scotland and Ireland. This is the biggest population to visit Britain and certainly the most widespread. Tucked away in the Solway estuary (OS maps 84 and 85), on the west-coast border of England and Scotland, is the entire breeding population of Spitsbergen. This population was once dangerously low with only some 400 individuals but it has now increased to several thousand and continues the same regular migratory flight. The third population to visit Britain's coast does so more as a straggler, and this comprises the Russian birds from the island of Nova Zemlya which normally winter in the Netherlands, having lost their German site through drainage. Extreme cold weather on the European mainland will force these delightful Geese to move westwards and it is then that the east coast birdwatcher can enjoy the spectacle usually only found in western Britain.

60cm

Black Grouse
Tetrao tetrix

Favouring moorland areas where these adjoin farmland and forestry, the Black Grouse is to be found in the more upland areas of Scotland and Wales, although northern England, the Peak District (OS maps 110 and 119) and Exmoor (OS maps 180 and 181) all hold small numbers. It is a traditional game bird, however, so that populations are often maintained by releases into the wild. This British bird has a truly remarkable breeding display. The males have traditional sites, many of which have been used for fifty years or more, known as leks, at which they gather and display communally. These display grounds attract the attention of the females by the sheer intensity of the males' activity. In the winter months the males attend the display ground at first light but, if snow is deep or temperature low, then there is little or no activity. A mild February day, however, will stimulate extensive display with males fanning and raising their tails to exhibit the spread of white feathers beneath while the wings are half spread and drooped. The display is accompanied by much crowing and hissing. This extraordinary behaviour can become so intense and preoccupying for the birds that there is even a record of one of the most frequent of its predators, the Goshawk, feeding on a female Grouse beside the lek while the males continued apparently unawares.

60cm

Red Grouse
Lagopus lagopus

At one time the Red Grouse was considered to be the one species of bird that was confined to Britain and occurred nowhere else in the world. The 'Willow Grouse', however, a variable species which is circumpolar in the northern hemisphere, is now considered to be the same species and the British Grouse is just a geographical race. A bird of the heather moorlands, the Grouse is confined to the north and west with small, introduced populations on Dartmoor and Exmoor. The great sporting interest in this bird, with extensive Scottish estates maintained almost entirely for it, has resulted in very detailed studies of the Grouse's life history being undertaken. In addition, a considerable amount of work is carried out to keep the heather areas in prime condition for the maximum number of birds. A visit to the Grouse moors on a bright February day will reveal the males indulging in their highly vocal display. The calls consist of a series of barking notes which are traditionally thought of as saying 'go-back, go-back, back-back-back', the string of notes speeding up as the bird reaches its climax. The bulk of the birds, however, are still in their winter coveys and, when disturbed, they explode into flight with a whirring of wings that takes them rapidly away, usually hugging close to the heather tops.

40cm

Pheasant

Phasianus colchicus

Originating in Asia, the Pheasant has been successfully spread throughout the world. The Romans are credited with much of this spread through Europe, but it was probably considerably later that the species was introduced into Britain. The Normans probably made the first introductions but it was several centuries later that the species became widespread. Populations and distributions are now highly variable because many birds are reared in captivity to be released to swell the wild stock. The modern Pheasant, with its close association with man, can be very tame especially away from shooting areas although it was originally a bird of dense cover, and rather shy. It is now very cosmopolitan and, although it is still found in the traditional thickets, open farmland, country parks, and coastal marshes all seem to provide homes. Reed beds have become very much a winter haunt and a rather unexpected February sight can be a small party of Pheasants exploding from the water's edge in a situation more in keeping with ducks. The earliest birds to be introduced and become established in Britain were from the western end of their natural range near the Caspian Sea. These males were rather dark and lacked the white neck ring that is a feature of the more recent examples introduced from the China end of the bird's range. From the eighteenth century, these later introductions have interbred with the earlier birds, so that the discovery of a male without a white neck ring is now a very rare event indeed.

65cm

Turnstone

Arenaria interpres

Our February birdwatcher must remain on the coast but forsake the vast open expanses of sand and mud and concentrate more on the stones, pebbles, and seaweed-covered rock if the most Turnstones are to be encountered. Breeding in the far north, this is a true winter visitor which may be found anywhere around the coastline, although the largest concentrations of more than 1000 birds occur in Shetland (OS maps 1 to 4) and Morecambe Bay (OS map 97). No bird could be more appropriately named because, throughout the feeding day – and Turnstones only seem to be inactive for a short period at the highest of tides – the bird is always searching for food. The technique is quick, simple, and efficient using the rather short, stoutish bill to flick over any likely looking stone, seaweed, or other rubbish on the beach. As the birds of a small feeding flock of Turnstones hunt rapidly for the hidden sandhoppers and other food items on the top of a February tideline of seaweed thrown up by the latest winter gale, they send a steady stream of sand and weed over their shoulders.

23cm

Rock Dove
Columba livia

33cm

On the remotest sea cliffs of western Ireland or north-western Scotland can be found some of the last remaining Rock Doves of true blood. Even here, unfortunately, the escaped or wandering domestic pigeon can attach itself to a winter flock and introduce the wide range of colour forms into the population. The Rock Dove is the wild ancestor for the whole spectrum of domestic pigeons and doves, from the fastest racer to the more bizarre ornamental. Stray racing pigeons are quick to return to the wild, often appearing in large numbers in urban situations or on coastal buildings, but also establishing themselves in sites previously occupied by the truly wild Rock Dove. If these pigeons were left to their own devices, the population would slowly revert to the typical Rock Dove plumage but the steady and increasing addition of exotic-plumaged individuals prevents this from happening. Ireland's battered Atlantic coast is a far cry from a London construction site or a small island in the Firth of Forth but all hold breeding populations of 'Rock Doves'. In common with pigeons everywhere, mild weather will produce early nesting in February although many birds are still with their winter flocks exploiting food supplies such as sandwich crumbs by a park bench or spilt grain on a cliff-top farm. A birdwatcher lucky enough to be among apparently genuine Rock Doves will find them surprisingly inactive for, after feeding, they will sit on a suitable cliff-face ledge or crevice and survey the scene below.

Tawny Owl
Strix aluco

Almost as familiar as the call of the Cuckoo *(Cuculus canorus)* or song of the Skylark *(Alauda arvensis)* is the childhood-learnt phrase, 'tu-whit, tu-whoo', that can be heard over a considerable distance on a calm, crisp February night. Absent from Ireland, the Tawny Owl occurs throughout the remainder of the British Isles inhabiting a wide range of sites from squares in the centres of large cities, where it feeds on birds such as Sparrows *(Passer domesticus)* and Starlings *(Sturnus vulgaris),* to the more typical deciduous woodland places, where the diet is principally small mammals. February is the first full month of song with males hooting regularly to establish their territories and females frequently answering. This is one of the most nocturnal of the owls and it is difficult to see but, during the winter, with leafless trees, the presence of a roosting bird is often disclosed by the assembled mobbing group of small birds, particularly tits, Robins *(Erithacus rubecula),* and finches which are apparently only too pleased to point out their discovery. As it sits pressed tight against the trunk of the roosting tree, the discovered Owl seems to treat its discoverers with the utmost contempt and continues its daytime sleep. If, however, it is forced to fly, then the mobbing birds give chase and their cries reach a new crescendo.

38cm

Carrion Crow
Corvus corone

The Carrion Crow occurs in two subspecies that are unusual in that they are easily distinguished by most birdwatchers and have been given quite separate names, the Hooded Crow and Carrion Crow. Very roughly, the Carrion Crow is found in western Europe and much of Asia, the Hooded Crow in northern and eastern Europe extending into western Asia. The British Isles has a resident population of both subspecies: the Hooded Crow in Ireland, Isle of Man, and northern and western Scotland; the Carrion Crow throughout the remainder of the country. All the British birds are resident but the Scandinavian population of Hooded Crows is migratory. They move south to avoid the severe winters and small numbers find their way across the southern North Sea. By February, this scattered population has settled into suitable wintering areas, almost always on the coast between Kent and the Scottish border, and often these birds remain tideline scavengers throughout their stay. The Hooded Crow differs from the all-black Carrion in having a grey body contrasting with the black of its head, wings, and tail. In flight, the grey underwing is most apparent. The zone where the two subspecies meet, overlap, and interbreed in Scotland produces a bewildering variety of hybrids with many examples appearing to be exactly half Carrion and half 'Hoodie'.

46cm

Rook
Corvus frugilegus

Although it resembles superficially the Carrion Crow, the adult Rook differs in having a slightly finer, less vicious-looking bill, a bare face, and ragged feathering or 'trousers' over the tops of its legs which are most apparent when the bird is walking. In flight, the Rook has a distinctly loose-feathered appearance with very ragged wing tips. Unlike the Carrion Crow, the Rook is highly communal both as a breeding species, when it is often in huge colonies, and also during the winter months when large numbers will congregate, often with Jackdaws *(C. monedula)*, to feed on open farmland and assemble in collective roosts, usually in woodland and often where the breeding colonies are to be found. The first eggs are unlikely to be laid in southern England until mid-March, and slightly later further north, but the colonies are full of activity throughout February especially if weather conditions are mild. With much noisy squabbling and mock fights, the old nests, that have remained from the previous year and stand out starkly in the tops of the leafless trees, are patched and played with. New sticks are added and old ones are stolen from the unattended nests of neighbours. Indeed, an unclaimed nest will be completely dismantled and added to those of the surrounding pairs.

46cm

Dipper

Cinclus cinclus

This is one of the most specialized of birds in its behaviour but it is widespread on upland river sites in all areas of Britain. The fast-flowing waters with gravelly or rocky river beds attract this plump, white-breasted bird which likes to sit on prominent rocks, often in mid-stream, and bobs continually with a rapid dipping movement, It feeds by diving beneath the water's surface to collect food as it 'walks' on the bottom, and Dippers are often readily seen through the clear waters seeming to be enveloped in a bubble of air. Territories are maintained throughout the winter but activity and song increase at the beginning of the year. By February, the Wren-like song, with its loud calls and trills, will be sounding clear above the continual background noise of tumbling water. By the middle of February nest building will have started and some pairs may even have eggs before the end of the month. The large domed nest is often built under a bridge or other man-made structure, frequently occupying the space left by a missing brick which provides a suitable cavity. Natural sites are holes in banks, particularly beneath overhanging tree roots or some similar shelter, but, most famous of all, are the birds which choose to nest behind waterfalls, appearing to fly directly into the sheet of water to reach their nests.

18cm

Mistle Thrush

Turdus viscivorus

The Mistle Thrush is the largest of our thrushes with the boldest of habits. It is also known as the 'Storm Cock' because it sings regularly in full voice from the most exposed of positions at the height of a storm. Song will start very early in the year and, if the weather is reasonable and mild, not only will song be reaching a peak in mid-February, but the bird will also be sitting on eggs. It is absent only from the northern isles of Scotland and it is a particularly pugnacious species throughout its range. Even when not breeding but at times of colder weather, the Mistle Thrush will attack any other species that may approach its 'protected' food supply. Disappointed householders putting out food to feed large numbers of birds in hard winters find themselves feeding a Mistle Thrush which is keeping all other birds away. At such times, and also when defending nests with eggs or young, Mistle Thrushes may not confine their attacks to birds. Cats are common victims of enraged Mistle Thrushes but humans, too, can suffer and the severe blows which the birds deliver can be all the more effective if the attack comes unexpectedly from an unseen direction. During the course of such an attack it is not unusual for the bird to draw blood from the person's scalp with its bill.

27cm

Pied Wagtail

Motacilla alba

Although this wagtail is present as a breeding species throughout the British Isles, the position is very different in the winter months when those from Scotland and the north of England move south, many of them leaving Britain to winter in the Mediterranean region. The birds from southern Britain are more likely to stay, remaining near their nesting sites and favouring lowland meadows near rivers, farmyards, open playing fields, and so on. In February, many of the communal roosts reach their peak in numbers of birds, although they can be occupied from early autumn until the following spring.

Sites vary greatly but reed beds are a

18cm

popular choice although clumps of bushes or dense waterside vegetation are also used. In recent years Pied Wagtails have increasingly tended to roost in heated greenhouses where large numbers can enter through the air vents. Such easily accessible roosts have enabled detailed studies of the species to be undertaken, and large numbers of birds have been trapped and ringed to study the subsequent migrations and life histories of individuals. In addition to the greenhouses, many larger cities now have winter Wagtail roosts in trees in the centre squares where the temperature is significantly higher than that of the surrounding countryside.

Hawfinch

Coccothraustes coccothraustes

The Hawfinch is a rather unusual-looking finch with a massive bill and short tail which give it a very 'top-heavy' appearance in flight. For its size and bulk, it is a surprisingly secretive bird and, although the species is widespread throughout much of England, the numbers are small and the birds difficult to detect. The greatest abundance is in the south-east, particularly the counties around London where the deciduous woodlands, open parkland, and orchards prove most attractive. If the breeding birds are difficult to find, the winter birdwatcher may be lucky enough to locate one of the flocks which are usually at peak numbers in February and likely to be encountered at any of the possible breeding sites. Numbers up to twenty or thirty are not unusual, but exceptional records have referred to gatherings of as many as 400. At this time of the year Hawfinches will also roost communally, and small parties may gather together most often in very dense cover near the canopy or in a particularly thick hedge. In all cases the birds are best located by the distinctive clicking note, somewhat resembling the call of a Robin – in suitable areas all 'Robins' calling from the very tops of the trees are worth investigating!

18cm

Yellowhammer

Emberiza citrinella

In winter the Yellowhammer is very much a bird of farmland, often in flocks feeding on exposed ploughed fields. Although Yellowhammers will mix with other finch species, this bunting is more inclined to keep in flocks or small parties of its own species. Severe frosts or snow will induce them to move into areas nearer the farm buildings where the presence of livestock will provide a ready food source, or on to the snow-free ground among orchards. Even in the hardest of weather, however, they are still likely to avoid mixing with other species. In mild Februarys, Yellowhammers will begin their breeding cycle. The winter flocks break down and they desert the open fields for the more vegetated sections of the farm or leave the area altogether in exchange for lowland heaths and commons. With mild weather attempts at spring song in late January will develop into full song by the end of February when the series of tinkling notes, expressed as 'little bit of bread and no cheese', is delivered from an exposed perch on the top of a bush, on telegraph wires, or on a wall. Only from parts of the Highlands and islands of Scotland is the Yellowhammer missing as a breeding species. Elsewhere it is widespread with an estimated population of nearly a million pairs.

16·5cm

Snow Bunting

Plectrophenax nivalis

A cold February day on the north-east coast of England and, among the scrubby grass above the high tideline, a flickering flock of birds is disturbed, flashing white in their wings as they fly off with a rippling, twittering, musical flight call. These are winter visitors, Snow Buntings from the north European breeding grounds in Scandinavia and Russia. Some birds from Icelandic sites may be found at this time on the west coast, but their numbers are small compared to those in the north and east. Almost any underdeveloped coastal area from the north of Scotland to the east of Kent will hold a small but annually varying population. Peak counts occur at times of autumn migration – a flock of 1000 individuals has been recorded – but the numbers present in February vary from year to year and, only in seasons with high numbers, are they often recorded along England's south coast. Although the entire length of the east coast is available and the species can be encountered throughout, two regularly used sites are at Gibraltar Point, Lincolnshire, where a bird observatory operates (OS map 122) and on the north Norfolk coast at Salthouse (OS map 133).

16·5cm

MARCH

The gravel pit in southern England is showing many signs of the rapidly approaching spring. Hawking the surface in a sheltered corner where the willow catkins are hanging over the water, are two Sand Martins freshly arrived from their southern wintering grounds. These are among the earliest of the summer visitors to arrive and, because they are dependent upon flying insects, they are rather susceptible to late cold spells but, if all goes well, not long after their arrival they will be inspecting the holes in the sandy bank, excavating new nest sites or revitalizing the old holes that have collapsed since last year. In complete contrast, some of the winter ducks have still to depart and a small flock of Shoveler, the drakes with their striking green heads and chestnut sides, are indulging in a typical mutual feeding activity. In unison the birds stretch their necks along the water, the broad bills resting on the surface and, as the flock moves forward, food items are sifted as water is allowed to flow through the bill. Elsewhere, ever-busy parties of Teal are dabbling in the muddy margins, again the males resplendent in

their full breeding plumage and occasionally interrupting the feeding to indulge in slightly quarrelsome chases as the pairings are sorted out for the coming breeding season. The majority of these ducks will be leaving in the coming few weeks, departing for the nesting grounds of northern and eastern Europe. The large rafts of Pochard and Tufted Ducks have already dispersed and the Coot have become increasingly quarrelsome and aggressive as they establish their own territories around the fringes of the pit, each seeking to hold the most favoured site. Among all this activity one striking display stands out. In the centre of the pit two Great Crested Grebes, in full breeding plumage with the striking orange to black head tufts, are indulging in the highly ritualized pairing display. To begin the two birds face each other with tufts raised and shake their heads. Then, separating, they both dive to surface again holding weed. They swim rapidly together until, breast to breast in the water, they rise up, appearing actually to stand on the water before sinking back again.

Great Crested Grebe *Podiceps cristatus*

The story of the changing fortunes of the Great Crested Grebe is as different as its strange displays which can be seen on large numbers of freshwater pools during March. The latter part of the nineteenth century saw a dramatic decline in the population because of a massive shooting campaign to serve the fashion industry. Fortunately, on one or two private waters, small numbers of Grebes survived and, with the introduction of more enlightened bird protection laws coupled with a change in people's attitude, the population began to rebuild, with a quite remarkable recovery by the early years of the twentieth century. Most freshwater lakes, reservoirs, or ponds throughout Britain except at higher altitudes, now have continually growing populations with birds successfully rearing young in some quite urban sites subject to considerable disturbance. March is the time to witness one of the most amazing displays in the bird world, with actions from the Grebes that have been labelled the 'head-shaking ceremony', the 'penguin dance ceremony', and the 'cat display'. Careful observations of a displaying pair will record both birds diving, surfacing with beaksful of weed, swimming rapidly towards each other, and rearing up vertically out of the water breast to breast. The birds then subside and quietly shake heads at one another before swimming apart and repeating the entire process.

48cm

Fulmar *Fulmarus glacialis*

The Fulmar is now one of the most familiar seabirds of rocky coasts and cliffs throughout the British Isles and, even where it is not breeding, birds can often be seen flying close to the cliff-face making use of every available updraught to play on the wind. Virtually unknown as a breeding species in British waters at the start of the century, a truly astonishing increase has led to a complete colonization of suitable sites on the British coast. The reason for this dramatic growth in numbers is still not fully understood. Birds will first prospect a site, often for several years, in advance of nesting, and individuals may be present and resting on the cliff throughout the summer. The new colonists are in occupation from the start of the year and are well established by early March, often behaving in a manner that makes it extremely difficult to know if they have laid eggs. They are extremely long-lived birds with life-spans in excess of thirty years, so that the species can continue to increase even though only a single egg is laid and Fulmars do not reach maturity until they are over six years old.

47cm

Teal

Anas crecca

The Teal is a breeding species throughout Britain, with a much enlarged winter population when immigrants from Europe and arctic Russia swell the numbers to some 50 000 individuals. An even bigger number winters south and west of the British Isles and it is in March that these birds start their return journeys. Most of the wintering birds have departed, but the migrants can be encountered on any area of shallow floodwater or on small vegetated ponds. The Teal cannot be confused with any other common duck because of its small size. In flight, the very rapid wing beats coupled with extreme agility, twisting and turning, often swinging low over the ground also help to distinguish it. Small parties are given the collective noun 'spring' which is a very accurate description of how the birds leap vertically from the water into the air when disturbed. Even the voice of the male is easily separable from that of other ducks, for it is a most unduck-like, low but rather whistling 'crick-crick'. The female has a more typical duck-like quack. A sharp-eyed birdwatcher in March should be on the lookout for the American race, known as the Green-winged Teal. The male of this species is easily separated from the European Teal by its vertical white line on each side of the breast but no white stripe on each side of the back.

32cm

Shoveler

Anas clypeata

March is Shoveler migration month when the birds are on their return journey to the breeding grounds of eastern Europe. Only some 500 to 1000 pairs remain to breed in Britain and are mainly concentrated in the south and east. This area also holds the peak of the March migration with some 200 in the Medway Estuary (OS map 178) providing the maximum at a coastal site. Shoveler are very much freshwater ducks, often occurring well inland with March counts exceeding 400 on the Ouse Washes (OS map 143). The quite extraordinary bill of this bird is put to good use when feeding and, unlike other ducks, Shovelers often feed in formation. Each bird extends its neck and head along the surface of the water, the broad bill stretched out in front allowing the water to filter through steadily. In this way food items are slowly sieved and strained from the water's surface. This feeding behaviour can often be indulged in by large concentrations of the birds swimming round and round in very tight circles.

50cm

Goldeneye

Bucephala clangula

Although the Goldeneye is confined to the lochs of the Scottish Highlands as a breeding species, small numbers winter on freshwater sites throughout Britain, and parties of up to twenty are not unusual. March is the month in which the black-and-white plumaged males indulge in the striking communal courtship display while still on their wintering ground. The display will continue throughout the migration, remaining at high intensity even when the birds are back on the breeding site. These displays usually involve several males gathering around one or two females and begin with rapid swimming as the males circle the females. The head of each male is drawn down between its shoulders and its body is raised out of the water by the very fast paddling. As the intensity of the display increases, individuals will often stretch their necks upwards and then take flight with fluttering wing beats, only to crash back into the water with much splashing. Finally, the drake throws his head backwards until the nape of the neck rests on the back with the bill partially open and pointing skywards. This is achieved with a quick jerking movement and then held for a short period. In an exaggerated form the movement is accompanied by much kicking and splashing with the feet.

45cm

Sparrowhawk

Accipiter nisus

The resident Sparrowhawk population in Britain has undergone some dramatic changes in recent years. Sparrowhawks were once widespread and common, but the population was kept in check by intensive keepering until the early 1940s when wartime activities allowed it to increase. The mid-1950s saw a major decline in the numbers of Sparrowhawks as a result of pesticides, and there was no recovery until restrictions on the use of certain chemicals allowed the population to regain its former abundance. Still absent from some areas in the east, the Sparrowhawk is now the commonest bird of prey in some northern and western sites although it is far less obvious than the more familiar Kestrel *(Falco tinnunculus)*. It is a more secretive species, preferring the dense thicket or open ride to the open country. The short, broad, rounded wings and long tail are well designed to give the bird great manoeuvrability when in pursuit of prey, or when it is twisting or turning among the trees. A favourite hunting technique is to fly rapidly along a hedgerow, suddenly rising and diving down on the opposite side of the hedge in an attempt to capture a small bird unawares. By March the pairs are on the breeding ground and often indulge in aerial display flights which take the bird through a pattern of slow, deliberate wing beats with a deeply undulating flight.

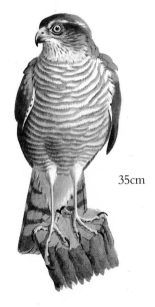

35cm

Goshawk

Accipiter gentilis

The Goshawk is the larger cousin of the Sparrowhawk, and is still a relatively rare breeding bird in Britain although small numbers now nest in several counties. Virtually all breeding sites are carefully protected because the eggs are still of interest to the egg collector, and young birds may be taken for hand rearing. The total British breeding population may be as high as forty to fifty pairs and a slow increase seems to be taking place since regular nesting was first recorded in the late 1960s following the Goshawk's virtual disappearance from Britain. It is considered likely that this recolonization is the result of escaped or deliberately released falconers' birds, the majority of which would have originated from European breeding grounds. It is possible that one or two recently reported birds, apparently nesting, are of the slightly larger and darker-crowned North American subspecies. Again, these could be escaped falconry birds even though members of this subspecies have appeared as genuine vagrants. An early-breeding species, much of the display is completed in February and it is not unusual for pairs to have eggs by late March, having finished the nest building or refurbishing earlier in the month. The usual site for the nest is the strong fork of a tree and, with continual use in successive years, a large amount of material can accumulate.

55cm

Red Kite

Milvus milvus

Historically, the Red Kite was one of the species that scavenged the streets of London in the days of open sewers and readily available rubbish. It is now confined to the oakwoods and valleys of central Wales (OS map 147) where a population of some forty pairs is resident. The main food source is now the dead hill sheep, and an animal carcass can often attract a small collection of carrion feeders including not only the Red Kite but also Ravens and Buzzards *(Buteo buteo)*. The Red Kite must be one of the easiest of the soaring birds of prey to identify, with its long forked tail and the rather long, ragged, and distinctly angled wings. In good light the tail can appear translucent with a distinctly reddish tinge. This tail is used to control the prolonged soaring flight and it is almost continually in motion, opening and closing, and twisting and turning in response to every slight change in wind and air currents. Although these Welsh birds are resident, migrants from southern Scandinavia and Germany occasionally occur in south-east England during March.

60cm

Lesser Black-backed Gull

Larus fuscus

Among the commoner gull species to occur in Britain, the Lesser Black-backed is unusual in being primarily a summer visitor. Small and slightly increasing numbers now over-winter, particularly in the south, but the majority departs for the Mediterranean basin southwards. March signifies the time for the birds to return with a steadily increasing number appearing throughout the country. Much of the migration takes place over land because, in addition to parties congregating at coastal sites, large numbers are recorded resting on open farmland, playing fields, reservoirs, and so on. This is the only large gull at this time to mix with the other two common inland gulls, the Black-headed and Common *(L. ridibundus* and *L. canus),* and the dark mantle, yellow legs, and tall stance all serve readily to distinguish the species. Some of the birds are en route to their Scandinavian breeding grounds rather than to the largely northern and western coastal sites of Britain. These Scandinavian birds comprise a distinct subspecies which differs in having a back that is as black as the wing tips, whereas the back of the British species is grey and contrasts with the black of the wing tips.

54cm

Common Gull

Larus canus

As a breeding bird, the Common Gull is confined to Scotland and Ireland where scattered colonies or individual pairs nest as readily at inland sites beside lochs or marshes as they do at coastal habitats. The Common Gull bears an unfortunate name because it is only in winter that large numbers of the extensive continental breeding colonies move westwards to winter in British waters. Although many Common Gulls spend the winter by the coast, this is the second most numerous gull, after the Black-headed, to roost and feed at the wide range of inland sites that gulls now exploit. A small isolated breeding colony of up to twelve pairs still attempts to nest at Dungeness, Kent (OS map 189) where the species enjoys special legal protection. These few pairs, which are almost certainly from the nearby continental colonies, enjoy only limited breeding success and their future cannot be assured even though they attempt to exploit a large range of nest sites from islands and open beaches to the tops of bushes. March sees the return migration of the birds heading for the Scandinavian breeding grounds, and large-scale temporary congregations appear on many open sites, both coastal and inland, as a marked movement takes place across the country. It is mainly the adult birds which take part in this cross-country passage while the immatures, perhaps returning for the first time, are unlikely to breed until a year later, and favour a more coastal migration line, often in concentrated streams passing steadily all day.

41cm

Sandwich Tern

Sterna sandvicensis

The Sandwich Tern is the largest and earliest of the terns to reach our shores each spring. This is one of the first of the summer migrants to be sought by the south-coast birdwatcher each March. The majority of the colonies are in the north and Ireland but the waters of the English Channel provide the gateway to the North Sea colonies on the East Anglian coast and further north on the Farne Islands (OS map 75). There are two very early records on the Sussex coast in February but most early stragglers arrive in the first half of March and most birds arrive from mid-March onwards. Originally named after the town of Sandwich on the Kent coast, this species was, unfortunately, soon lost as a breeding bird in that county. In recent years, however, considerable developments on the RSPB's Dungeness reserve (OS map 189), with the construction of islands within a large freshwater complex, has resulted in a recolonization of the county, and a nucleus of regular breeding birds is now present. Although they are unlikely to be seen regularly over the nesting islands until April, Sandwich Terns are on the nesting areas from March onwards, and the establishment of viewing hides has made observations at Dungeness particularly easy.

41cm

Barn Owl

Tyto alba

The Barn Owl is worldwide in distribution except that it is absent from much of Asia apart from India. It is certainly one of the most familiar of owls and one that attracts considerable folklore. The Barn Owl is particularly active and vocal in March, and the bird's variety of hisses and shrieks has given it the alternative name of 'Screech Owl'. From its plumage, it has been called the 'White Owl'. In flight the bird seems to be almost all white, and the most frequent sightings are in the headlights of cars when the whiteness is greatly exaggerated. Unfortunately, the bird is highly prone to road accidents and many are picked up injured or killed. The call, whiteness of the plumage, and the living quarters in old barns, church towers, and so on have no doubt resulted in the origin of many country ghost stories. The strange noises and floating ghostly white shapes around church yards can give rise to strange yarns. Very occasionally the Barn Owl can literally 'glow' in the dark, which obviously enhances the telling of any tale! This phenomenon even seems to give rise to some accounts of UFOs! The explanation is probably quite simple; living in holes in trees and buildings the Owl's plumage has become polluted with luminous bacteria that are normally found on the decaying wood.

35cm

Sand Martin

Riparia riparia

Occasionally, individual Sand Martins will remain in Britain throughout the winter but this early-arriving member of the swallow family is usually recorded for the first time each spring in early March and, by the end of the month, it has become widespread throughout the country breeding in virtually every county where suitable habitat is to be found. Unlike other members of the swallow family, the Sand Martin does not build complicated structures of mud attached to buildings, but excavates its own nesting burrow in a suitable sandface such as a river bank or, more often, in a commercial sand quarry or gravel pit. The presence of men, noise, and heavy machinery and equipment apparently has little effect upon the breeding success of the birds and may even add to their security. Highly colonial, not only does the species sometimes nest in dense colonies of several hundred pairs but, before and after the breeding season, large communal roosts will gather in reed beds throughout the country. A co-ordinated research programme of trapping and ringing birds at these roosts has shown how they move about the different sites after arriving in the spring and before autumn departure. This work also produced an indication of the very dramatic decrease in the population in the late 1960s, the result of the exceptional droughts in the Sahel region which is the wintering ground of British Sand Martins.

12cm

Magpie

Pica pica

In the mid-1600s a small flock of Magpies found its way across the Irish Sea and arrived on Ireland's east coast. The birds found the countryside to their liking and the Magpie is now an extremely common Irish bird. The total population is probably descended from that one small flock in the seventeenth century. Elsewhere in Britain, the species is found everywhere except in the far north of Scotland and, although numbers are small in some areas, such as East Anglia, elsewhere it is a particularly common species which is becoming more and more urbanized. Larger gardens, parks, and squares in many of the cities now hold breeding Magpies. They can be particularly damaging to other nesting birds and they also raid bird-tables, food deliveries, and so on. An early-nesting species, the nest building, undertaken by both adult birds, is well underway by mid-March. The nest differs from that of the other crow species in its domed construction which adds to the security. Although nests are usually built in inaccessible places, they can often be very low down just off the ground but, in these circumstances, they are usually in the middle of dense cover. The chosen site can be tenaciously adhered to and there are recorded examples of nests under construction being knocked out of the bush but rebuilt daily until the human tired rather than the bird!

46cm

Long-tailed Tit
Aegithalos caudatus

March is nest-building time for this tiny bird with the long tail. Individuals are never seen alone, and Long-tailed Tits are usually found in small flocks. They look rather like bumble bees with tails attached as they move along a hedgerow or through the woodland, with their perpetual buzzing calls serving to keep all members of the flock in contact. The remarkable nest structure of these birds has given Long-tailed Tits various country names, including 'Bottle Bird', 'Feather Poke', 'Two-finger', 'Barrel Tit', and 'Poke Pudding'. Building work is carried out by both adults, producing a ball of fathers and hair with a small entrance hole (just large enough for two fingers) tucked away almost invisibly in a bramble thicket or overgrown hawthorn. The work involved in the construction is extensive; both birds bring material and work from within the nest turning round and round accumulating vast quantities of feathers that are held together with cobwebs. The nest is disguised on the outside with a layer of lichen. A careful examination of nests at the end of the breeding season indicates that it is not unusual for a pair to have used more than 2000 feathers in the making of a single nest. Destined to hold as many as twelve eggs or even up to twenty on rare occasions, the structure must be particularly secure to hold that number of growing young.

14cm

Black Redstart
Phoenicurus ochruros

The Black Redstart has a chequered British history. At one time a rare winter visitor, the Black Redstart is now a regular breeding species in small numbers and an even more regular migrant, particularly in the south-east, on spring and autumn passage. March is the time to search for this bird on the south-east coast, because this is when an adult male in striking plumage may be encountered on its return journey to the German breeding grounds. The rather drab grey of the female and young bears no comparison with the magnificent black body, red tail, and prominent white wing flashes of the male, displayed to their fullest as the bird perches on exposed rocks and fences. Although there were early isolated breeding attempts, and small numbers of pairs nested in the south-east in the 1920s and '30s, it was not until London and other south-eastern towns had suffered wartime bombing that the Black Redstart increased its population by exploiting bomb sites in the centres of cities. Although bomb sites have now gone, large-scale construction sites, power stations, factories, and so on have all provided alternatives. The Black Redstart is still very much a bird of the south-east, but England can now boast a regular population of some thirty to 100 pairs.

14cm

Dartford Warbler   *Sylvia undata*

On the southern mainland of Europe, the Dartford Warbler is a widespread species inhabiting a wide range of scrubland. As a non-migratory, insect-eating warbler it cannot survive in the more northern or eastern areas where winter food is absent. Because of this, the species holds a rather precarious position in southern Britain occupying the heather and gorse heaths of the southern counties from Sussex to Devon, and particularly favouring areas around the New Forest and the Dorset heaths (OS maps 195 and 196). The population is never large and it is generally under threat from the fragmentation of its delicate heathland environment. Severe winters can result in heavy mortality, particularly if snow cover is persistent, and heaths that lose their breeding populations may not easily become repopulated. In 1961, for example, the total British population was about 460 pairs but, following the cold winter, only some 100 pairs could be located. A second severe winter in 1962/63 further decimated the breeding birds and, at the very most, there were only twelve pairs in the whole of southern England in 1963. Fortunately, with ten years of mild winters, a recovery to nearly 600 pairs had taken place by the early 1970s. And March is the month when the bird starts to sing, before most of the migrant warblers have arrived.

12·5cm

Cirl Bunting   *Emberiza cirlus*

The Cirl Bunting has undergone a dramatic decline and contraction of range in recent years. It was once common throughout much of southern England and Wales, and it was even considered to be more numerous than its close relative the Yellowhammer in some parts of its range. It is now virtually restricted to the south-west in Devon and Cornwall. In song throughout March, the rattling trill has been likened to a Yellowhammer's song but lacking the final flourish and it probably resembles more closely the rattling song of a Lesser Whitethroat *(Sylvia curruca)*. The male bird, singing from the topmost twigs of a convenient tree or exposed overhead wire, is unmistakable with his green breast-band, black throat, eye stripe, and crown, with contrasting yellow on the remainder of his face. The striking white outer tail feathers are very apparent in flight or as the tail is flicked while the bird is feeding on the ground. The less boldly marked female is very similar to the much commoner and more widespread Yellowhammer, but differs in having a greener less yellow head, and browner, less chestnut rump. Overall, the Cirl Bunting appears slightly smaller and squatter than the Yellowhammer.

16·5cm

APRIL

The leaves have opened just enough to hide the previously bare limbs of the trees, but still not enough to close completely the canopy and, as a result, fingers of sunlight shaft through the wood in a summer-like welcome to the first of the migrants to start arriving. Most of our summer visitors do not put in an appearance until early May but, in the second half of April, the woodlands begin to fill with song. The resident species have been singing for some time but the distant drumming of one of the spotted woodpeckers always attracts attention. The drumming sound is produced by striking rapidly a piece of dead timber with the bill – a mechanical song and one which carries a considerable distance through the wood. Other woodland songs at this time of year are also rather different from the normal singing. That familiar herald of the spring, the Cuckoo, appears in southern England from the middle of the month and, by late April, a woodland walk will almost certainly be accompanied by its distinctive voice. Also by the month's end, the first of the Turtle Doves are back in the woods. Unlike our other pigeons which are all resident, this is a summer visitor travelling to wintering grounds south of the Sahara each year. Equally unlike our other pigeons is the voice, not one hint of a 'coo', more an imitation of a 'trim phone' purring in the wood. During a warm late April evening in an English wood, the local rookery is extremely noisy because the birds now have young and there is a continual coming and going. Towards dusk a certain stillness settles, a solitary Willow Warbler still sings its descending song, and the surprisingly warm April evening air is filled with the purring of Turtle Doves. In a small clearing an early litter of fox cubs comes out to play, chasing one another around until complete darkness and silence descend upon the entire wood. Even the local Tawny Owls make no noise, but suddenly the night air is filled with the voice of the finest of British songsters, the Nightingale. Sweet, mellow, and varied, the Nightingale's song can be heard regularly during daylight, but it will always be at its best during a solo performance in the still of night.

Bittern

Botaurus stellaris

The Bittern is a highly specialized bird, confined to dense reed beds, and its distribution in Britain is dictated by the distribution of its habitat. Two well-known RSPB reserves which hold breeding populations are Minsmere, Suffolk (OS map 156) and Leighton Moss, Lancashire (OS map 97). The presence of birds in an area, however, is no guarantee that they will be seen because the Bittern is a secretive species, and lucky indeed is the birdwatcher who may catch a glimpse of them in flight keeping low above the reed beds. The birds prefer to feed where reed and water meet and many flights are made as the birds move to and from their feeding grounds. Recent management work within reed beds, however, has created open water and ditches which has reduced the amount of movement that the birds need to make. In April the breeding birds are vocal, with a strange, resonant booming call which vibrates around the reed bed. The call is not loud and it is repeated at intervals of a few seconds for four or five times, but it has amazing carrying power and will often be quite audible as much as 4 kilometres from the bird. More persistent booming takes place at dusk and the rather ventriloquial nature of the call often makes it difficult to decide in which area of reeds the bird is hidden.

75cm

Eider

Somateria mollissima

The Eider is a highly marine species. The striking black-and-white plumage of the male makes him unmistakable, but the drab brown coloration of the female and young male is much less eye-catching. Confined as a breeding species to the northern coasts, the majority of females have settled on to their eggs by the end of April and, at this time, the drab coloration fulfils the important need for camouflage. The females show very little fear of man and sit very tight on the eggs under a small clump of vegetation or pressed against a suitable log or other debris. In some areas it is quite possible to stroke the sitting bird or even to lift her gently from the eggs to examine the nest contents – not that either is to be recommended because this can clearly point the way to the sitting bird for any potential predators. Most of the Eiders have departed from southern waters by April, but a small number of immature non-breeders remain in small parties in one or two sheltered coastal sites. The majority of these are in the all-dark-brown plumage of the full immature, but among them will be a few young males approaching maturity and, then, they can exhibit a bewildering mass of patchy brown, black, and white feathering.

59cm

Red-breasted Merganser

Mergus serrator

Until 1950, the Red-breasted Merganser was a breeding species confined to Scotland and Ireland where it nested on overgrown islands in lakes and lochs. Often the vegetation around the nest is so dense that the female virtually has to construct a tunnel to and from the water's edge. The clutch of some eight to ten eggs is laid towards the end of April and, at this time, the males form single-sex flocks on the lake and have nothing further to do with the rearing of the young. Very occasionally, however, a male has been recorded accompanying a female with newly hatched young. Since the early 1950s, the species has spread southwards into north-west England colonizing the Lake District, and has continued to spread further south and into North Wales. Coupled with this has been a movement eastwards into the Peak District and neighbouring Yorkshire. This diving duck is very much a fish-eating species, both on the breeding grounds and in its more maritime winter quarters on any coastal water, estuary, or sheltered bay. The long, thin bill with the serrated edge is ideal for grasping food items from eels to salmon and small cod. This diet does not endear the bird to fishermen and, in the past, large numbers of Mergansers have been shot, although this has not prevented the continued spread.

58cm

Golden Eagle

Aquila chrysaetos

This is Britain's only nesting eagle and, as one of the larger eagles, it is probably the most widespread and commonest in the world. In Britain it is confined to the Highlands of Scotland, although one or two pairs nest in the Lake District and pairs have nested on the coasts of Northern Ireland. The population has enjoyed varying fortunes in recent years, and has suffered pressures from toxic chemicals which are used in sheep dips, egg collectors, as well as baits positioned to kill other predators such as crows in grouse-rearing areas. The Golden Eagle seems to be surviving, however, and protection schemes and surveys undertaken each year guarantee the survival of some young. A much improved attitude towards large birds of prey has removed some of the pressures which dictated that any bird with talons and a hooked bill had to be destroyed. The Golden Eagle is an early nester, and many of the eggs will be hatching towards the end of April. Although two and sometimes three eggs comprise the normal clutch, in virtually all nests, only the first egg to hatch survives. The single young takes two or three months to fledge and is then dependent upon adults for a further three months, so it is well into the autumn before the adults' breeding responsibilities have been completed for the year.

80cm

Little Ringed Plover *Charadrius dubius*

Before the very first breeding record in Britain in 1938, the Little Ringed Plover was an extremely rare migrant visitor with only some sixteen authentic British records. From the late 1940s the species became more and more familiar as the number of breeding pairs increased and the population almost exploded from just a handful of pairs near London to reach a total of about 400 pairs stretching as far north as the Clyde. The species remains a summer visitor, returning during April to inhabit a wide range of man-made sites from slag tips and sewage farms to reservoirs although it favours particularly gravel pits. The species is so used to the close proximity of man and working machines that little seems to deter the nesting attempt, and any clutches that happen to be lost are readily replaced. On arrival the males immediately begin to display with much calling and flighting around the breeding ground making their presence at the site especially obvious. These breeding grounds are often shared with the slightly larger and more numerous Ringed Plover, although this remains principally a coastal species. The smaller Little Ringed Plover differs in having a higher-pitched, almost monosyllabic call note, no white wing bar in flight, paler legs, smaller head, and, when it is viewed at close quarters, it shows a prominent yellow eye ring.

15cm

Golden Plover *Pluvialis apricaria*

Breeding on the high ground in much of the north and west, including some areas in western Ireland, the Golden Plover makes a complete change of habitat in the winter months. Then the birds move southwards and abandon the moorland tops for the lower-lying meadows and flood plains of lowland Britain which they share with large flocks of Lapwings (*Vanellus vanellus*). The total population is greatly swollen by immigrant birds from further north. In April, the return migration is in full swing, with many birds that have wintered further south from the continental mainland stopping over on English marshes and pastures. At this time many of the birds have acquired their breeding plumage, having completed their spring moult before leaving the winter quarters. In this summer dress it is possible to separate the two distinct geographical subspecies. The 'southern' form, which breeds from Ireland to southern Scandinavia, has black restricted to the breast and belly, while the 'northern' form, with breeding grounds stretching from Iceland to central Russia, has black on face and throat as well, with the black surrounded by a distinct white band. Both of these forms are identical in winter plumage.

28cm

Black-tailed Godwit   *Limosa limosa*

Historically, the Black-tailed Godwit was a widespread breeding species throughout much of England, favouring the wet meadows and grazing pastures where cattle left suitable grass hummocks to provide shelter for the incubating birds. A combination of several factors, but probably including extensive land drainage, shooting, and egg collecting, resulted in the complete disappearance of the species as a breeding bird in the early 1800s. In more recent years the numbers at traditional wintering grounds, such as the Shannon Estuary in Ireland where over 8000 birds have been recorded, have been increasing. Coupled with this increase there has been a return of the breeding population. Since 1952 nesting has occurred annually at the Ouse Washes, Cambridgeshire/Norfolk (OS map 143) which now hold a thriving population, while small isolated colonies or breeding attempts take place in many counties from Kent to Shetland. In April, the birds are back on their breeding grounds. They have a most distinctive display flight which shows the broad black-and-white barring on wings and tail to great effect. The highly vocal birds rise at a steep angle with beating wings, then fly with short, clipped wing beats on very bowed wings before gliding silently downwards to alight with up-raised wings.

40cm

Bar-tailed Godwit   *Limosa lapponica*

Unlike its close relative, the Bar-tailed Godwit is a winter visitor and passage migrant only, the birds originating from the breeding grounds of Scandinavia and western Russia. Well over 50 000 individuals winter at British coastal sites, for the species is rare inland. From October to February the estuaries on the west coast, around the Irish Sea, hold some of the largest concentrations. By April the majority of these birds have departed and most can be seen on the east coast with several thousands still present on The Wash (OS maps 131 and 132). At this time many of the birds have acquired the rich, chestnut-red summer plumage on the underparts while some are still in the full grey dress of winter providing a marked contrast between individuals in the same flock. The spring passage includes many birds that have wintered further south on the African coast in Morocco and, with a wind from the south or south-east in late April, many of these can be seen flying past the headlands of Beachy Head, Sussex (OS map 199) or Dungeness, Kent (OS map 189). Over 4000 on one day have been recorded moving past in an easterly direction as large flocks stretched out over the sea.

35 cm

Little Tern

Sterna albifrons

The Little Tern is the smallest of the British terns, and it is a strictly coastal species favouring the shingle and sandy beaches as a breeding site. Unfortunately, however, it has suffered severe losses in recent years with a marked contraction of range and desertion of several breeding colonies, particularly in the south-east. Egg laying is unlikely to take place until May but the feeding birds are off-shore by the breeding sites in late April. Pairs sit side-by-side on the beach, courtship feeding, with the male presenting the female with small fishes. The small size, yellow-and-black bill, white forehead, and rapid wing beats serve to separate the species from other terns, while the regular hovering on rapidly beating wings with down-pointed bill is a distinctive feeding technique. A major factor in the decline of the Little Tern is that it favours beaches which are also popular with holidaymakers. Natural predators, however, such as foxes, large gulls, and stoats have all seriously depleted the Tern's numbers while, at many sites, the eggs are regularly lost to the high spring tides. Protection schemes are in operation in many areas, with electric fencing protecting nests from foxes at Rye Harbour, Sussex (OS map 189) and chalk banking providing sites above the tide at Tetney, Lincolnshire (OS map 113). Unfortunately, the continuing activities of egg collectors still adversely affect this species.

24cm

Turtle Dove

Streptopelia turtur

Unique among the British pigeons, the Turtle Dove is a summer visitor, spending the winter south of the Sahara in tropical Africa and returning to Britain between mid-April and mid-May. Large numbers are regularly shot for food on their migration through the Mediterrean region but, unlike the other pigeons, this species escapes the attentions of the shooter in Britain and receives the full protection of the law. The distribution is very much south and east, with only small numbers to be found in the south-west peninsula and Wales, and very few records from Scotland and Ireland. The purring song of the newly arrived birds is a clear harbinger of summer and can be heard among the trees and scrub near open farmland. Turtle Doves feed on the ground and exploit farm crops, including particularly some of the ripening cereal crops. They are smaller and lighter than most other pigeons, and they are able to reach the heads of growing corn. One of the densest breeding populations occurs in the RSPB's reserve at Northward Hill, Kent (OS map 178) where over seventy pairs can occur in little more than 50 hectares.

27cm

Great Spotted Woodpecker

Dendrocopos major

Apart from in the northern isles and Ireland, the Great Spotted Woodpecker is widespread throughout Britain. It has become an increasingly familiar bird as its habit of feeding from garden bird-tables has spread and, for some individuals, become daily routine. As well as attacking the hanging peanuts and coconuts, the species has also discovered the milk bottle, perhaps from observing the feeding behaviour of tits. For a bird accustomed to excavating holes in trees it is a simple task to open a bottle and sample the cream. The presence of a bird in a particular area is usually indicated by the distinctive 'tchack' call note that carries far through the woodland site. There seems to be little preference for particular tree species, the birds appearing to favour mixed woodland plots which often contain deciduous and coniferous trees. During April the drumming of the Great Spotted Woodpecker can be heard resounding through the woodland territory. Serving the same function as a vocal song, this drumming noise is produced by rapidly beating the tip of the bill against a dead log or tree branch which functions as a sounding board. The only other British woodpecker to do this is the Lesser Spotted *(D. minor)* which produces a quieter but longer drumming.

23cm

Crested Tit

Parus cristatus

For a species with such a wide distribution, virtually throughout continental Europe, it is surprising that this should be the rarest and most local of the British tits. Confined to the Highland woods of Scotland, a favourite site is in the valley of the River Spey (OS maps 35 and 36). Recent years have seen a small increase and spread of the species which may be the result of increasing commercial forestry plantation or the extensive provision of nest boxes which are readily used. As with one other British tit, the Willow Tit *(P. montanus)*, the pair must excavate their own nest site so that the nest box should be filled with expanded polystyrene to enable the birds to dig out their 'cavity'. This is a highly sedentary species and, although Crested Tits mix with other tits in the winter months, they rarely move far from the breeding grounds. By April the very characteristic purring trill can be heard, immediately identifying the presence of the birds, while the sounds of individuals excavating a nest hole in rotting wood may give away the probable nest site.

11·5cm

Redstart

Phoenicurus phoenicurus

14cm

The Redstart is quite widespread in Britain but the population is densest in the west although, surprisingly, it is extremely rare in Ireland. Typically it is associated with open oakwoods adjoining areas of grazed farmland with stone walls. Redstarts are among the earlier summer migrants to return and many are on the breeding grounds by April. Eggs will not be laid until May but the song, courtship, and nest site selection are all completed before the end of April. The male will sing from an exposed perch among the open woodland from which fly-catching flights are regularly undertaken when the flashing red of the tail is most apparent. Before nesting, courtship chasing is a regular feature of the display, with the male chasing the female in the vicinity of the eventual nest site. The birds regularly use nest boxes and, although a standard tit-style box can be occupied, the birds prefer the box to have a larger hole. It should also be slung beneath branches to produce the effect of a natural hole in a broken bough. Natural nesting sites in trees are most regularly used but a wide variety of alternative sites can be available, ranging from cavities in stone walls to ground sites such as holes in grass banks.

Nightingale

Luscinia megarhynchos

Mid-April and the woodlands, scrub, and coppice of south-east England is suddenly filled with nocturnal song. The Nightingale must be one of the best-known British birds, rivalling the Cuckoo and Swallow *(Hirundo rustica)* as a harbinger of summer. One or two birds have still to arrive by early May but, by the third week of April, most of the regular sites have recorded their first singing Nightingale of the year. Although the song and name are familiar, the bird is a rather unimpressive individual and would probably be passed unnoticed by many of the people who are fascinated by the song. The Nightingale is a little bigger than a Robin, and appears to be a bird of uniform brown plu-

16·5cm

mage with a richer red-brown tail. The song is delivered from well within cover and the bird is often completely invisible although patient waiting and observation will often disclose its whereabouts. Coppicing is less often practised these days and, unfortunately, this type of woodland is the bird's favourite habitat. The RSPB reserve at Wolves Wood, Suffolk (OS map 169) and the extensive woodlands around Canterbury, Kent (OS map 197) hold substantial breeding populations.

Sedge Warbler
Acrocephalus schoenobaenus

13cm

Many migrant bird species do not arrive in Britain until early May but several, including the Sedge Warbler, put in an appearance from mid-April onwards. By the time the later arrivals appear, the Sedge Warbler is already widely spread throughout its breeding range. This is a common bird of the dense vegetation in damp or wet areas, favouring the edges of gravel pits, marshes, and reed beds. The distinctive churring, chattering song is delivered from a prominent perch or in 'parachuting' song flight where the bird flutters vertically upwards and then descends on raised wings. The closely related Reed Warbler *(A. scirpaceus)* uses purer stands of reeds for nesting, but the two species often feed in the same habitat. Their songs are also similar, although the Reed Warbler's is more repetitive. Visually, the Sedge Warbler differs in having a broad, creamy stripe above the eye and a well-patterned, streaked back. It also lacks the strongly rufous rump of the Reed Warbler.

Whitethroat
Sylvia communis

14cm

April is the first arrival month for Whitethroats in Britain. Before 1969, the Whitethroat was the commonest British breeding warbler with virtually every hedge and piece of scrub throughout the country holding breeding birds. The breeding season of 1968 was good and large numbers of young were reared. The autumn migration of that year, studied at the British bird observatories, also indicated a normal population level. In the spring of 1969, however, very few Whitethroats appeared, not just in Britain but elsewhere in western Europe as well. It was estimated that nearly 80 per cent of the total population had been lost since the previous autumn. Subsequent investigations considered all possible causes, ranging from disturbed meteorological conditions during one of the two migrations south of Britain, excessive use of persistent toxic chemicals on the wintering grounds, and so on. Although the species has shown some small signs of recovery, it has never approached the former population levels. It is thought now that the cause of this major decline has been the severe droughts in the southern Sahara region of Africa, the species' main wintering area. It is surely more than coincidental that the serious droughts started in 1968.

Lesser Whitethroat   *Sylvia curruca*

Like so many of our summer migrants, the first of the arriving Lesser Whitethroats appear in mid-April with the remainder of the population in residence by mid-May. One major difference from the bulk of our summer visitors, however, is that in the autumn the species migrates south-eastwards and passes around the eastern end of the Mediterranean to its African wintering grounds. The bulk of the migratory species, including the closely related Whitethroat, migrates through Iberia and past the Mediterranean at its western limits. This is very much a bird of the south and east of England; it is scarce in Wales and the south-west, almost absent from Scotland, and there are no breeding records from Ireland. The Lesser Whitethroat is often skulking and not easy to see but the characteristic rattling quality of part of the song is very reminiscent of a Yellowhammer or Cirl Bunting. Although it only forms part of the full song, it is the section that carries over the greatest distance. Visually, the Lesser Whitethroat differs from the sightly larger Whitethroat in having a generally greyer plumage, lacking any chestnut, and showing distinctly darker grey ear coverts which give it a masked appearance.

14cm

Goldfinch   *Carduelis carduelis*

Occasionally, Goldfinches lay eggs in April but most breeding starts in May and many birds are still in flocks during April. Very appropriately the collective noun for Goldfinches is 'charm' but, because Goldfinches are popular with the cage-bird breeder, many alternative names for the birds have originated in different parts of the country, including 'cheveril', 'King Harry', and 'thistle finch'. The latter is particularly apt, because the structure of the Goldfinch's bill, broad at the base but coming to a fine point, is very suitable for exploiting its favourite food items, including the seeds of various thistles and the teasel. Indeed, the Goldfinch is the only species of finch that can reach teasels' seeds which are positioned at the bottom of long tubes. Observations have shown that the males, which have slightly longer bills than the females, can exploit this food source more readily, and parties feeding on teasel clumps are probably largely males. It is not unusual for finch flocks to consist of a single sex and most of the April Goldfinch flocks probably conform. Although it is difficult to see the small differences in the lengths of the bills, the red face on the male extends behind the eye whereas, in the female, it stops level with or even in front of the eye.

12cm

MAY

Sitting on a heather-and-gorse-covered knoll in the late afternoon, we can see the purple and yellow of the heath stretched out across the valley down to the distant pond where the water had been so useful for the fire fighting in the year of the drought. It now plays host to numerous bright-blue dragonflies that hawk back and forth close to the water's surface. A nearby male Stonechat is calling with the harsh persistent note that indicates it is annoyed at having its territory disturbed by a human intruder. A short distance away a Tree Pipit is parachuting downwards in full song flight to land on a lone pine tree. There is no sign of the Sparrowhawks that are known to be nesting in the isolated clump of pines on the other side of the valley but, in the distance, the liquid, musical notes of a Woodlark can be heard and we make a mental note of the direction so that we can investigate on a later visit. The sun turns to a fiery red as it moves into the last half-hour of its day when, out of the sky, a Hobby comes scything across the heath like a giant Swift. The rapid flight is halted and the bird begins a slow and graceful gliding and circling over the distant pond. A sudden dash, a rapid turn and twist of the tail, and a dragonfly is plucked from the air, and then, with slow gliding flight, the Hobby makes off across the heath, deftly removing the wings from the insect and feeding itself from the talons as it goes. In that last hour of daylight when the sun has disappeared but darkness has not quite descended, the Grasshopper Warblers start their rather monotonous reeling song that appears to leave them with no opportunity to take breath; a small herd of fallow deer breaches the skyline and a solitary Barn Owl floats ghostly white and in complete silence overhead. Darkness steadily creeps up and blocks out the scene but, with its arrival, comes the sound that we have been waiting to hear, the churring of the Nightjar. Highly adapted for a nocturnal existence, these birds are dependent upon the moths and other night-flying insects and, but for their most distinctive of songs, their presence would so easily go unrecorded.

Great Northern Diver *Gavia immer*

The Great Northern Diver is the largest of the diver species and is also the only non-breeding member of the group to be found regularly in British waters. Most of the British birds originate from the Icelandic breeding grounds and, each year from May onwards, small numbers are found summering in the northern isles, particularly the Shetlands. In some years there are indications that the species may be nesting. At the same time, somewhat surprisingly, this is when small numbers are regularly recorded on passage in the English Channel. The main wintering grounds are on the west coast, and Great Northern Divers are particularly numerous on the Irish Seaboard. Small numbers winter in France and the English Channel, however, apparently returning to their breeding grounds via the North Sea. Each May small numbers are reported from headlands such as Dungeness, Kent (OS map 189) or Cap Gris Nez on the French coast, moving eastwards before their eventual northward passage. The Great Northern Diver can usually be easily distinguished from the more common Black-throated *(G. arctica)* and Red-throated species by its greater size, thick, heavy neck, and slow, powerful wing beats. In flight, the large feet protrude prominently and the birds seem more like Cormorants *(Phalacrocorax carbo)* in size and bulk. In full summer dress, the black of head and neck, together with the white-patterned back are equally distinctive features.

77cm

Common Scoter *Melanitta nigra*

The Common Scoter is a rare British breeding species, but one of its most regular sites is Lough Erne, County Fermanagh, in Northern Ireland where a population of some 100 pairs nests in most years. In May the flocks have arrived on the breeding lough and small parties or pairs are starting to haunt the edges of the islands that will be their eventual nesting sites. At this time the species has changed habitats completely from marine to freshwater. Common Scoters gather for the winter in many sheltered coastal bays or estuaries where they can feed on marine molluscs and, on their return migrations, large flocks, strung out along the horizon, move steadily northwards. Most of these movements have been completed by mid-May, although small numbers of non-breeding birds summer on their wintering grounds. A rather non-descript, uninteresting-looking duck, the all-black coloration of the male is only relieved by the orange on the bill while the brown female has prominent pale cheeks and, in flight, contrasting pale underparts.

45cm

Goosander

Mergus merganser

Unlike its close relative the Red-breasted Merganser, the Goosander is a freshwater species at all times of the year, often remaining on or near its breeding ground throughout the winter. It is also one of the very few hole-nesting species of ducks. By May Continental immigrant Goosanders have deserted their wintering grounds of southern England where they haunt the man-made reservoirs, gravel pits, and canals, and are only found on the breeding sites of northern Britain and Wales. Any upland water area with a suffficient food supply will be colonized, from the smallest rushing stream, that seems more suitable for a Dipper, to a large mountain lake. The males with their striking, creamy white plumage and dark-green head are near the breeding site or nesting tree for a very short period of only a few weeks. After that they assemble in all-male flocks on some larger area of water to undergo a plumage moult. The female is left to rear the young, including sitting on the ten or so eggs in the hole of a convenient waterside tree and, eventually, leading the brood to a safer site during fledging. In areas where the species is common, several broods will congregate to form large parties of young.

67cm

Hobby

Falco subbuteo

May on an area of southern heathland and, at dusk, a Hobby with its dashing flight could well come scything across the sky. This small falcon is a truly summer visitor, departing our shores completely in the winter months and returning each spring to exploit an abundance of large flying insects as well as aerial-feeding birds such as Swallows and martins. The total population is not large, only some 100 to 150 breeding pairs confined to southern England. It is one of our rarest breeding raptors and, unfortunately, it is still a prize much sought after by the egg collector. Observations on feeding birds show that Hobbies change their habits markedly as the season progresses. When they first arrive in May, they eat mainly insects, particularly flies or larger moths, although flying ants, beetles, and so on are all taken as the bird sails and hawks over open country. Insects are caught in the talons, and then transferred to the bill and eaten in flight. Later in the season, and particularly when there are young in the nest to be fed, the diet changes to birds, and spectacular chases in pursuit of pipits, larks, Swallows, or even Swifts *(Apus apus)* take place. Unlike the insects, birds are normally carried to a plucking post where they are stripped of their feathers before being eaten.

35cm

Quail

Coturnix coturnix

During late May in a rolling grassland field on the chalk hills of southern England, the distinctive voice of the Quail can be heard calling from somewhere among a rough, tussocky patch of grass. This rather strange, far-carrying, and highly ventriloquial call has been likened to the words 'wet-my-lips' or 'but-for-but' and, once it is heard it is never forgotten. The presence of a calling bird is not indicative of breeding, because unmated males often call persistently for several days before moving on. Confusingly, however, once a male has mated he will stop calling. Trying to stalk a calling bird is extremely difficult; although the Quail may never seem far away, it appears to be almost impossible to creep any closer to it and it always just a few metres further on. The British population fluctuates widely, and the reasons for declines and falls or superabundance in a 'Quail-year' are not fully understood. Changes in farming techniques as well as shooting in the Mediterranean region, must play their part in a possible decline but, when suddenly in a particular spring, large numbers of Quails arrive, it can only be because of some change in the meteorological pattern bringing them from further east.

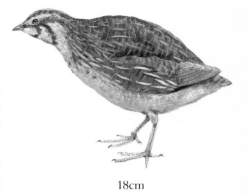

18cm

Ruff

Philomachus pugnax

The Ruff on the display ground or lek must be one of the most fascinating and certainly the most colourful of all the British breeding waders. Historically, it was a widespread nesting species in eastern and southern Britain but, in common with so many of our marsh birds, the increasing drainage and intensification of agricultural methods resulted in its loss as a breeding species. It remained a regular migrant, with small numbers wintering in Britain, but the nearest nesting birds were in the lowland areas of Denmark and the Netherlands. Since the early 1960s a small recolonization has taken place with a regular population at the Ouse Washes, Cambridgeshire and Norfolk (OS map 143) and one or two other isolated sites. During May the lek is at its height and the males, with their strikingly coloured ruffs, engage in mock battles observed by the females. During these battles the cock bird raises the feathers of its head tufts and neck ruffs to display a striking circular pattern from face on; the birds run backwards and forwards chasing, pecking, and, occasionally, flying upwards face to face with feet kicking. Observations have shown that the strongest males and most frequent winners of these battles are the ones that mate with the females.

25cm

Whimbrel

Numenius phaeopus

Very few British waders are summer visitors and completely desert our shores during the winter months. The Whimbrel winters in Africa south of the Sahara but, by mid-April, the first of the returning birds are back in Britain and the peak passage occurs in early May. Evidence from ringing shows that individuals follow the same route in successive years, and have traditional stopping points where they will frequently remain for several days before continuing northwards. Many passage birds head for nesting sites outside the British Isles, but a few make for the northern islands which comprise the only British base. Shetland provides the densest population, and here the birds can be seen displaying over the breeding moorland by mid-May. Each bird circles its territory on rapidly beating wings giving the distinctive bubbling trill. The call also serves to separate the Whimbrel from the closely related, similar, but larger Curlew *(N. arquata)*.

41cm

Pomarine Skua

Stercorarius pomarinus

The Pomarine Skua was once thought to be a very rare bird in Britain partly because the rarer skuas are difficult to identify but also because few birdwatchers gazed out to sea in search of birds. It breeds in the arctic regions of America and Asia, and there is only a very small north European population. Otherwise it is a highly marine species that is only likely to be seen from some prominent headland or off-shore island and only then if the weather drives the birds closer inshore than usual. Once considered commoner in autumn, observations in recent years have shown a marked spring passage in early May and this movement has been noted at a wide range of sites from the south-west corner of Ireland to the Outer Hebrides in the west, and even at points such as Beachy Head, East Sussex (OS map 199) or Dungeness, Kent (OS map 189) in the south-east. Watching for the May Pomarine Skua passage has now become an annual event and the numbers regularly passing our shores are considerably higher than the older bird books would suggest. A spring adult carries a very distinctive tail, with the central feathers elongated and twisted into a club shape at the tip. Smaller than the Great Skua *(S. skua)* which shows broader more rounded wings, the Pomarine is larger and heavier than the more familiar Arctic Skua *(S. parasitica)*.

50cm

Arctic Tern

Sterna paradisaea

The Arctic Tern is, quite rightly, famous for being the bird that undertakes the longest of all avian migrations. Some individuals spend the breeding season in the short summers of the high arctic only to migrate southwards following the oceans to a winter in the antarctic. They arrive in British waters from late April onwards and there is a steady passage throughout May and early June. Although a few scattered pairs nest among the closely related Common Tern *(S. hirundo)* colonies at coastal sites in the south-east, this is very much a bird of the north and west. Apart from a few inland colonies in Ireland, the population is almost entirely coastal. By the end of May the birds are back on the nesting grounds and many have eggs. The Arctic Tern is a truly colonial species and many of the more northern sites in the Orkneys and Shetlands contain tens of thousands of birds so that separating them from the equally numerous Common Terns in the area can be extremely difficult. The Arctic has shorter legs, a longer tail, greyer body plumage, and a uniform dark blood-red bill without a black tip. The bill changes to all-black at the end of the breeding season.

36cm

Nightjar

Caprimulgus europaeus

During a calm, warm evening in late May on the sandy heaths of southern Britain, the sound of a churring Nightjar can fill the air. Scattered pairs breed as far north as Scotland but the area from Devon to Norfolk is the stronghold of this nocturnal summer visitor. Always a bird of mystery, the list of country names is extensive and a clear indication of its nocturnal habits and rather owl-like appearance: 'fern owl', 'churr owl', 'night chur', or 'night hawk'. The name 'night hawk' refers to its somewhat hawk-like appearance if it is flushed by chance during daylight. Another alternative name, 'goat sucker', stems from the belief that the bird would suck the milk from sleeping goats or cows during the hours of darkness. In fact, its huge mouth is ideally adapted for catching night-flying insects. May is the time of arrival from the African wintering grounds and, although voice and display are at their peak at this time, the birds will often continue calling until well into August after the breeding has been completed. Two eggs are laid in a small clearing or on the edge of a fire break, and the bird sits tight throughout the day relying upon its cryptic coloration for camouflage.

27cm

Woodlark
Lullula arborea

The May song of the Woodlark is probably one of the most beautiful bird sounds of spring. Unfortunately, it is rather underrated because the species is now so reduced in numbers and distribution. In the past, Woodlarks could be found in most counties of England and Wales, as well as over much of Ireland which they have now deserted. The stronghold is currently the south-west although some numbers of pairs are still to be found on the heaths and brecks of southern England. The full song is less varied than that of the Skylark and lacks the dramatic delivery. The liquid, bubbling notes are far more musical, however, and are delivered from a prominent perch or a hovering song flight. The song consists of a series of short phrases combined into a varied sequence so that no two song bursts are exactly the same. A bird in full song will continue for an hour or more, each song sequence separated by a brief pause of a few seconds. Observations suggest that males occupy a territory and sing for up to six weeks before nesting begins and, with song continuing well into the breeding season, there is a particularly long song period. The Woodlark prefers open country and it selects a song post that dominates the territory and provides an all-round view of the close-cropped grass of the feeding grounds as well as the bordering areas of long grass and heather which provide the nest site.

15cm

Grasshopper Warbler
Locustella naevia

The completely unmusical, reeling song of the Grasshopper Warbler has been likened to the sound of an angler's reel as the line is being pulled out against the ratchet. Unfortunately the May birdwatcher is more likely to hear this Warbler than to see it for it is very much a skulking species associated with scrub and reed on the edge of wetland areas. The bird is highly vocal at night as well as during the early and late hours of daylight and then a patient watcher may be lucky enough to catch a glimpse of its rather nondescript, streaked plumage and very rounded tail. The song remains the key to the bird's presence, however, and will often continue for as much as two minutes or more with a strange mechanical quality. The high-pitched series of trilling notes carries a considerable distance, particularly in the still night air and, because the bird regularly turns its head this way and that, the song seems to vary in volume and is very hard to locate. The species is widespread throughout Britain and Ireland but there are local areas of high density and other areas where there are no Grasshopper Warblers. The population is continuously shifting in response to forestry activities because the birds prefer the scrub areas that occur during some of the earlier years following planting.

13cm

Reed Warbler

Acrocephalus scirpaceus

The Reed Warbler is one of the later summer migrants to arrive
each spring and does not put in an appearance until May. Indeed,
most birds do not arrive until the second half of the month.
Largely confined to the south of England, with just a few pairs in
Wales, this is one of the more specialized warblers as far as habitat
requirement is concerned. It does not need vast areas of reeds but
it is so closely associated with the plants that, even where it nests
in other vegetation, there are almost always some reeds nearby.
In many sites Reed Warblers are very colonial and, even where
reeds cover several hectares, the birds will often be concentrated
in groups in particular areas. Reed Warblers often seem to be on
the edges of the reed beds where the plants are standing in water
because it is here that they seem to find some of the best feeding
possibilities. Although reeds provide the main site, an early
morning visit to the area will show that at this time of the day, the
birds regularly leave the reed beds to feed where they can exploit
potential food sources in the scrub and bushes bordering the
marsh. Studies of this species have shown it to be one of the
longest-lived of all the small, insect-eating migrant birds to visit
Britain but, even so, about three-quarters of all the young birds
die in their first year, while some four out of every ten breeding
adults cannot expect to survive to breed another year.

12·5cm

Marsh Warbler

Acrocephalus palustris

Probably less than 100 pairs of Marsh Warblers now breed in
Britain each year, with well over half of these in the county of
Worcestershire. Clearly, it is one of the rarest of the regularly
breeding summer migrants. There has always been considerable
confusion in the identification of the Marsh Warbler away from
its main areas even when the birds are in full song in spring and
when they are most vocal following their arrival in late May and
into June. The Marsh Warbler is particularly well known for its
powers of mimicry and has a far more varied song than that of
the similar-looking Reed Warbler. One authority has recorded
some fifty different species of birds imitated by singing Marsh
Warblers including Partridge *(Perdix perdix)*, Green Woodpecker
(Picus viridis), various tits, Nightingale, and Magpie. Visually
there is very little difference between the Reed and Marsh
Warblers, particularly between young birds in the autumn. The
adult Marsh Warbler, however, lacks the rufous coloration
around its rump where is has a more olive tinge. It is not even
easy to distinguish the two species in the hand by close
examination of the feather structure. On the other hand, the
Marsh Warbler hangs its nest from the vegetation by basket
handles whereas the Reed Warbler weaves it into the reeds.

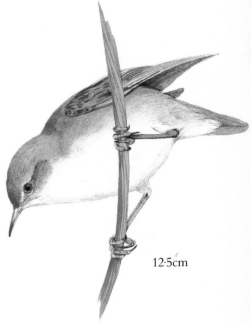

12·5cm

Garden Warbler

Sylvia borin

Although some of the returning Garden Warblers are back on their breeding grounds by mid-April, the bulk of the summer visitors do not arrive in Britain until mid- or even late May. This is probably because of the distance the birds travel, and many individuals will have wintered far to the south in Africa, even beyond the equatorial region. For British breeding birds, inhabiting woodland with associated scrub throughout much of England and southern Scotland, the migration route is via Iberia which they use as a staging post in spring and autumn. Before a migratory flight, the birds will store layers of fat to supply energy during the migration and the staging posts enable them to top up their depleted reserves. A normal weight for a Garden Warbler is slightly less than 20 grams but a record 37-gram bird has been reported from Nigeria in spring, when it was preparing to tackle the northward flight across the Sahara. It has been calculated that a bird carrying such a quantity of fat would be capable of flying more than the 4800 kilometres without stopping. This is perhaps one of the most confusing and difficult warblers to identify because of its lack of distinctive features. It has a short bill and round head, together with brownish-grey upper parts and pale buff underparts.

14cm

Wood Warbler

Phylloscopus sibilatrix

As its name suggests, this in indeed a bird of woodland, although it will often continue to return each spring to sites where woods have been felled or coppiced as long as some mature trees remain. Although the population is densest in the north and west, the species inhabits rather different woodland types in different parts of the country. The birds of the south and east favour mixed deciduous sites although a small number of conifers does not discourage them. In the north, birch woods are preferred and, in the west of England and Wales, it is the oak woods on valley sides that provide the main habitat. In some areas, apparently scattered colonies occur with several pairs inhabiting one part of the wood but seeming to ignore identical-looking woodland nearby. The characteristic song includes a distinctive trill, which has been likened to a spinning coil running down on a metal plate, and accompanies short flights on rapidly shivering wings or similar wing actions while perched. Once nesting has begun, and particularly when the birds have young, a distinctive piping call locates the pairs. The domed nest is placed on the ground and almost always has a suitable arch of twigs or small roots across the entrance.

12·5cm

Pied Flycatcher

Ficedula hypoleuca

Pied Flycatchers begin to arrive from the African wintering grounds in late April and begin the breeding cycle in May. It is very much a bird of the west and north, and it is particularly widespread in Wales. Occasional migrant birds appear on the east coast in May, but these are continental breeding birds which have drifted across the southern North Sea to make landfall on the English coast. They rarely stay more than a day before re-adjusting their migration back to the Scandinavian breeding grounds. The British breeding birds are hole nesters and, in many sites, particularly forestry situations where natural holes are absent, the number of breeding pairs has been significantly increased by the provision of nestboxes. The standard tit-style nestboxes, familiar in gardens throughout Britain, are readily used and, at RSPB reserves such as Nagshead, Gloucestershire (OS map 162) or Gwenffrwd, Dyfed (OS map 147), a substantial box population of Pied Flycatchers has been created. Indeed, within the area of its distribution, it seems only necessary to erect the boxes to obtain the Flycatchers! The staple diet, particularly when rearing young, is caterpillars from the oak leaves and, in years when these are very abundant, the normal flycatching behaviour is abandoned completely in favour of a more warbler-like feeding pattern.

13cm

Tree Pipit

Anthus trivialis

Absent from Ireland and the northern isles, this summer visitor is widely spread throughout the remainder of the country apart from some upland sites and particularly open areas such as the fenlands of East Anglia. In southern England it is not unusual for two broods of young to be reared in a single year so that, by mid-May, the eggs for the first clutch have been laid. Open country, heaths or parkland, or more open woodland sites are chosen where the bird can establish a high song post in a wide clearing. An isolated tree or even an electricity pylon fulfils this function and, as well as delivering the song from a perch, the bird will also make a song flight which carries it upwards in full song only to parachute back to the perch on quivering wings. The rather similar Meadow Pipit *(A. pratensis)* will also inhabit open country, although it usually prefers fewer trees. Its song flight starts and finishes from the ground. The Meadow Pipit has less yellow on the underparts and has dark legs rather than the pink of the Tree Pipit, as well as a much shorter hind claw!

15cm

Redpoll

Carduelis flammea

Since the early 1950s, the Redpoll has shown quite a dramatic increase in numbers and has spread throughout Britain. Particularly obvious has been the movement into southern England from the more traditional areas in the north although the south-west still has only a rather sparse breeding population. An excellent example of the marked increase in Redpolls in the south-east is provided by the Dungeness Bird Observatory (OS map 189) where the number of annual records for 1953-56 range from none to thirteen and in 1959-62 a massive 116 to 293. The Redpoll is distributed throughout the higher latitudes of the northern hemisphere and exhibits considerable geographical variation. Birds known as Arctic Redpolls are very much paler with pure white rumps and are generally considered to belong to a separate species although interbreeding does occur. The British birds are often referred to as Lesser Redpolls and are among the most southern of the populations. Egg laying can begin in early May making it possible for the birds to have three broods a year, which is impossible for the more northern Redpolls. The nest is rather large and untidy for a bird of this size; it is placed high in the fork of a tree or bush and, with a completed clutch, contains between four and six eggs.

Tree Sparrow

Passer montanus

The Tree Sparrow can be regarded as a rural replacement for the House Sparrow. It inhabits a wide range of sites where hole nesting is a possibility including trees, buildings, and quarries, but it is probably often overlooked. It is relatively scarce in the north and west although breeding birds do occur on some very remote marine islands as well as in a wide range of Irish localities. Because Tree Sparrows are hole nesters, they will readily take to nest boxes and, in woodland or other rural situations, a colony of Tree Sparrows will take all the boxes available, regularly rearing two broods and occasionally three. At the RSPB reserve at Northward Hill, Kent (OS map 178) some 200 standard tit-style boxes were occupied by Blue and Great Tits *(Parus caeruleus* and *(P. major)* early in the season and then taken over in late May by the large population of Tree Sparrows. In the years when the two species were out of phase in their nesting cycle, be it for climatic or other reasons, the tits would regularly lose in the battle for the boxes. The Sparrows could dominate by using larger amounts of bulkier nest material which they could collect more rapidly. There are several records of Tree Sparrows building nests on top of clutches of tits' eggs and, on at least one occasion, a nest was constructed on top of a brood of young tits still being fed by the adults.

JUNE

One hundred metres or more below, against the rocks at the foot of the vertical cliff, the ocean swell is bursting in a shower of white spray. Just clear of the spray and looking around with complete indifference is a lone Shag, recently having completed a fishing expedition and now resting with outstretched wings while, a few metres above, its mate is sitting on eggs hidden away within a rocky crevice which provides protection from the severest storm. Above the Shag a Rock Pipit parachutes downwards in song flight, the string of notes barely audible above the sound of the sea. Higher up the cliff face the birds are lined on the ledges as if in a tenement building in some overcrowded squalid street, with line upon line of individuals packed closely into each floor. The entire scene is shrouded in a swirling mass of giant white snowflakes which are the Kittiwakes passing backwards and forwards along the cliff face. They glide almost effortlessly on the upcurrents of air and seem simply to enjoy the experience of freedom of movement without physical effort – nature's very own hanggliders. Only a few days ago the same Kittiwakes were coming and going with beaks full of seaweed, but now nest construction is complete, eggs have been laid, and the off-duty birds have leisure time at their disposal. A careful look at this swirling mass of white, however, shows up an occasional grey bird with even more mastery of the air. Fulmars, with straight, unbending wings, pass swiftly among the other birds, showing their close relationship with the shearwaters and albatrosses as their control of flight is complete and their wing movements almost nil. It is extremely difficult to ignore the continual movement in the air but, out on the sea, easily riding the heavy swell are rafts of auks, dominated by the Guillemots, but including smaller numbers of Razorbills and Puffins. From time to time a bird takes flight, fluttering along the surface of the water, legs running rapidly to give added impetus, and short, stubby wings flapping with a whirring action until eventually the bird is airborne. Then to the cliff face, with the Guillemots settling on the narrow open ledges, Razorbills landing beneath the overhangs and in the crevices, and the Puffins tucking themselves completely out of sight within caves or holes in the rocks.

Gannet

Sula bassana

It is during June when the eggs in the gannetry are hatching, and the grey, rather reptilian-looking young lay naked and helpless in the bottom of the nest. Within a couple of weeks, however, the appearance of the chicks is transformed by the dense layer of whitish down that they have acquired. This too, will eventually be lost as the birds grow their covering of whitish-speckled, dark-grey feathers. Unfortunately, there are few places where the breeding cycle of the Gannet can be readily observed because, although the country holds more than 150 000 breeding pairs, almost all of them breed on isolated off-shore islands in the far north or west. This total represents nearly three-quarters of the world population and indicates just how important Britain is for the world's Gannets. Thoughts of Gannets conjure the exotic names of some of the remotest rocks, such as St Kilda, Bass Rock, Skellig, and Grassholm, places which to many must remain just names. Fortunately, there is one mainland site where Gannet-watchers can enjoy splendid views with no difficulty. From specially prepared, safety viewing points at the RSPB reserve of Bempton Cliffs, Humberside (OS map 101) a colony of over 200 pairs can be watched throughout the season from the earliest displays to the eventual fledging of the young.

90cm

Tufted Duck

Aythya fuligula

The large flocks of 'Tufties' that combine with Pochard *(A. ferina)* to sit in 'rafts' on areas of open water throughout the winter months disperse in March and April. In recent years there has been a rapid increase and spread of the breeding population as the birds exploited and colonized the growing number of gravel pits, reservoirs, and other freshwater sites during the 1950s and '60s in some areas of the south. The species now nests throughout Britain, apart from the extreme north and south-west, and the Tufted Duck has changed from being only a common winter visitor to one of the most numerous breeding ducks, even out-numbering the more familiar Mallard *(Anas platyrhynchos)* at some sites. In more urban situations, (and wild Tufted Ducks do breed in the middle of London) the birds can become extremely tame, readily accepting food from the hand as does the more familiar town species. This does not mean that these ducks have lost their natural wild instincts because Tufted Ducks, ringed in central London in the winter months, have been recovered from far into eastern Europe in the summer. The Tufted Duck nests much later than the other breeding species and the first small all-dark diving ducklings do not appear until mid-June. Unfortunately, although the broods are large, they are often severely predated by pike during the first few days after hatching.

43cm

Marsh Harrier

Circus aeruginosus

Although a few Marsh Harriers may remain in Britain for the winter months, the species is a summer visitor that is still one of our rarest breeding birds of prey. Each spring and autumn a small but regular passage of birds from the scattered European breeding grounds pass through south-east England, and a few birds remain to breed. The centre of British breeding is now East Anglia and, fortunately, most pairs reside on nature reserves. Some of the easiest viewing of Marsh Harriers is on the RSPB reserve at Minsmere, Suffolk (OS map 156) where observation hides allow splendid views of flying and hunting birds. The Marsh Harriers needs are quite specialized, for it is strictly a reed-bed bird and prefers the wet reed beds to the drier sites. The size of the site is not very important and the birds have bred successfully in some very small patches of reeds. Prospecting birds have often used ripening cereal fields where the reeds of a boundary ditch grow out into the corn and provide an uninterrupted expanse of reed-like vegetation. Not all summering birds are nesting pairs and often records in June refer to non-breeding, summering immatures that may even be seen flying with sticks and going through the motions of nest building and territory holding. A successful breeding pair may rear as many as six young which are fed largely on young birds such as Coots, or ducklings taken from the nearby water areas. In some areas, however, the food-collecting adults may range over the neighbouring farmland.

50cm

Osprey

Pandion haliaetus

The Osprey story is one of conservation's successes, is very well known, receives annual publicity, and yet bears retelling. In the last century the Osprey was a common breeding species in much of Scotland, nesting in trees by the many suitable lochs as well as on isolated crags. The eventual extinction of the British breeding population in the early years of the twentieth century can be blamed solely on human action. The number of Ospreys was controlled because of an apparent conflict with sporting interests and, as the numbers decreased, the actions of egg collectors and the desire for stuffed birds eliminated the final pair at Loch an Eilean. Since 1950, however, the Scandinavian population has been increasing and the numbers of migrants appearing in Scotland also grew with a single pair attempting to nest at Loch Garten in the Highlands. The first few years were somewhat disastrous, with disturbance from egg collectors and birdwatchers, but, with organized protection, this site is still occupied annually and breeding is successful in most years. There are now some twenty-five or more pairs of Ospreys in Scotland each summer and breeding success is good. Viewing facilities for the public are available at Loch Garten (OS map 36) and at Loch of Lowes (OS map 53).

55cm

Corncrake

Crex crex

The Corncrake population of Britain has undergone a dramatic decline within the present century. It was once quite widespread although it has never been very common in the south-east. Now it is absent from virtually all areas except parts of Ireland and Scotland. To hear the rather rasping and scraping call of the Corncrake on a fine June night, the birdwatcher must head for Ireland, the Hebrides, or Orkney and, even then, it is not certain that the journey will be successful. The Corncrake is more likely to be heard than seen, for it is remarkably secretive and, even careful stalking will not necessarily reveal the bird because its voice has a certain ventriloquial quality. The persistent, all-night calling is exciting for the visiting birdwatcher but it is often most frustrating for the local inhabitants who can be kept awake night after night! The Corncrake has suffered as a result of increasing farm mechanization because, when the bulk of the hay fields were cut by hand, the breeding birds could escape but, with machines cutting in June, the birds, nests, and young are all lost. The decline is also affecting western Europe where, if anything, the reduction has been even more dramatic to the extent that the 2000 or fewer pairs now breeding in Britain have gained major international importance.

27cm

Snipe

Gallinago gallinago

During June on some rough, flooded grass or marsh virtually anywhere in Britain, the sound of a drumming Snipe is likely to be background noise. The site may be an upland bog or a lowland meadow for all are used by the Snipe as long as the dry tussocks remain in which to hide the well-camouflaged nest and eggs which eventually hatch into very dark, white-speckled young. The drumming is unique in the bird world and is a mechanical noise produced by the stiff outer tail feathers which are carried at right angles to the body and are vibrated rapidly by the wind as the bird undertakes a diving display flight. This drumming or vibrating noise has been likened to the sound of distant bleating goat and has given the bird such local names as 'heather bleater', 'kid of the air', or 'bog bleater'. When the young have hatched, the behaviour of the adult birds changes. They are often to be found perched on a prominent post or gate giving voice to a persistent 'chipping' alarm call whenever danger threatens. In most cases the brood of four young is divided by the parents and they are then reared to fledging in isolation, so that the whole brood will not be lost to some passing fox.

27cm

Great Skua
Arctic Skua

Stercorarius skua

S. parasiticus

58cm

Skuas are equivalent to marine birds of prey. They occur over the deep oceans as well as over more inshore waters and they only resort to land for breeding purposes. In Britain breeding is confined to the northernmost parts of Scotland and predominantly to the islands of the Hebrides, Orkneys, and Shetlands. Their behaviour is piratical in that almost all their food supply is found by chasing other seabirds and forcing them to drop the food they are carrying or to disgorge their latest meal which might be done either in fright or as a means of discouraging further chasing. The smaller Arctic Skua most frequently chases terns or smaller gulls while the larger species concentrates on the large seabirds and even includes Gannets among its victims. There are records of the Great Skua catching hold of the wing of the target bird until the last meal is regurgitated. The disgorged food item is often retrieved in flight before it hits the water, a further display of the bird's aerial agility following a flying pursuit which has involved manoeuvres all over the sky. When breeding, both species are particularly active in the defence of their nests and young; they lay their eggs early in June and hatch broods towards the end of the month. All intruders are fearlessly attacked and even humans can be struck about the head with bill and wings if they wander too near the nest. Both species breed in close proximity although this has only occurred in recent years following a marked increased in the Great Skua population which was very low because of persecution. The Great Skua used to be favoured by the crofting community when it drove White-tailed Eagles *(Haliaeetus albicilla)* away from the newly hatched lambs but, with the departure of the Eagles, the Skuas lost their popularity. Now the bird is staging a recovery and is more numerous than the smaller species. The Arctic Skua occurs in two colour phases, light and dark, and, in both phases, the bird has elongated feathers extending from the centre of its tail. The wings are swept back and pointed, and the flight is extremely dashing. In the light phase the bird has a very pale neck and under parts with a contrasting dark cap and upper parts; in the dark phase the Arctic Skua is nearly uniform dark brown in colour with a trace of a white flash at the base of its flight feathers. It is in the dark phase that the species most closely resembles the Great Skua which is more like a short-tailed immature gull. The larger species has no colour phases and no tail projections; it is also a uniform dark brown while the broad-based, rather rounded wings show prominent white flashes at the base of the flight feathers.

57·5 cm

Black-headed Gull   *Larus ridibundus*

Gulls generally are among the most successful of all birds, and the Black-headed Gull in particular has exploited the success to the utmost. The term 'seagull' is no longer applicable because a high proportion of the population spends at least some of the year far from the coast and some of the birds probably never see the sea. Vast numbers of Continental Black-headed Gulls swell the British population in winter when it is a familiar sight in virtually all habitats taking food from rubbish dumps, city parks, freshly turned soil behind the plough, or from the beach at low tide. In June, however, apart from wandering first-year non-breeders, the birds are near their colonies. Scarcest in the south and most numerous in the north, the breeding sites are as various as the feeding stations and include coastal sand-dunes, off-shore islands, islands in gravel pits and reservoirs, and beside upland lakes and marshes. Colonies can be huge, with the largest at Needs Oar, Hampshire (OS map 196) containing some 20 000 breeding pairs, while the total British population must exceed 100 000, a marked change from virtual extinction during the eighteenth century. The dramatic increase in the numbers of this small, highly adaptable gull has put considerable pressure on the more specialized terns which are summer visitors and are now arriving to discover their nesting sites occupied by the earlier-breeding gulls. As a consequence, the management of gull populations is being closely studied in many areas because the rate of their increase is clearly the direct effect of man's activities.

37cm

Roseate Tern   *Sterna dougallii*

The Roseate Tern breeds on both sides of the Atlantic but its numbers are small and declining in the two areas. In Europe, Britain holds almost all the breeding pairs and the majority of these occur on nature reserves where they enjoy a certain amount of protection. Unfortunately, the species seems highly prone to suffer poor breeding success in years of bad weather, and the winter quarters on the west African coast hold even greater dangers because the birds are regularly trapped. All the colonies are on rocky or sandy islands which are usually off-shore, or in coastal sites. The numbers of colonies are falling as the species continues to decrease, with the most marked decline taking place on the North Sea coast, while the birds breeding in the Irish Sea area manage, at least at the moment, to maintain their numbers. At one site, Dungeness, Kent (OS map 189) small numbers have bred in recent years, the only real indication of the species exploiting new sites. Colonies are often mixed with the Common Terns', but the overall whiteness and more delicate appearance of this species is most apparent. The extremely long tail streamers give the bird a definitely elongated appearance and the rather slow wing beats produce a very buoyant almost bounding flight.

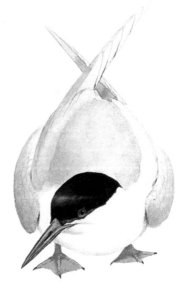

38cm

Razorbill
Guillemot

Alca torda

Uria aalge

Around sea cliffs in the north and west of Britain on a June day, the sky is full of the sights, smells, and sounds of auk colonies. The birds continually fly to and fro, some leaving to make their way out to sea for feeding, others arriving either just to sit or perhaps to take their share of incubating the eggs or delivering food to the young. Others just play on the perpetual updraught of wind along the cliff face apparently enjoying the ease of flying because normally the rather short, stubby wings have to be flapped extremely rapidly to maintain the birds in whirling flight. Although they are very closely related and often found at the same sites, the two species may be distinguished because of the blacker plumage and heavier bill with white crosslines of the Razorbill. They also choose different nest sites. Guillemots nest on open ledges where they pack themselves tightly together standing with their breasts pressed against the vertical cliff face, their tails protruding over the open drop to the sea below. The Razorbill seeks out the nooks, crannies, and crevices, often tucking itself away inside and out of sight, and rarely in such compacted numbers. Neither bird builds a nest but they lay their single, distinctly pear-shaped egg on the open rock. The shape is an adaptation that helps to prevent the eggs from falling off the cliff, because they roll round in a circle rather than in a straight line. There is usually a small number of 'bridled' Guillemots among the colonies; these are distinguished by their white eye rings and white lines extending backwards from these. The more southerly colonies have a lower percentage of bridled birds, with less than 1 in 100 present on the south coast but as many as a quarter of the total population in the most northerly colonies in the Shetlands. These bridled birds readily form pairs with unbridled individuals. In England the Razorbill and the Guillemot are found at the same number of limited sites in the south from the Isle of Wight westwards; in the north-east only at Bempton, Humberside (OS map 101) where excellent viewing facilities are available, and small numbers on the Farne Islands (OS map 75); on the west coast of England, St Bees Cumbria (OS map 89) also has viewing facilities at the colonies. Colonies are widespread on the sea cliffs of Scotland, Wales, and Ireland. Both species collect their diet of fish by diving from the surface of the water. This leaves the birds highly susceptible to contamination of the plumage by any floating oil and, although in some areas this is a regular occurrence in the winter months, the perpetual fear is that a major pollution incident will occur near a breeding colony and have a serious effect on the population.

40cm

41cm

Black Guillemot
Cepphus grylle

Britain is virtually the southern limit of this northern auk, and the Black Guillemot is very much a bird of the north and west. Unlike the other auks, this species is largely resident and remains in the area of the breeding site throughout the year. There is only one English station, the reserve at St Bees Head, Cumbria (OS map 89) where the RSPB has provided public viewing facilities although it is necessary to search the sea carefully to find the small numbers of pairs present. The north and west coasts of Scotland and the Irish coastline provide the stronghold of this species, with small numbers around the Isle of Man and Anglesey. In the more northern sites the bird is known most commonly by its old Norse name of 'Tystie' while, more recently, it has acquired the name of 'Pigeon Guillemot', from its rather rotund shape and overall pigeon-like appearance. Unlike the other auks, this species favours the rocky base of the cliffs among the boulders and caves just above the tideline, finding suitable nooks and crannies in which to lay its two eggs. In June, the birds are in their full black breeding plumage with prominent white wing flashes and brilliant red legs and feet. By contrast, the winter plumage is a rather mottled white, and the bird is rather untidy in appearance.

32·5cm

Puffin
Fratercula arctica

Here is one of the bird world's clowns, for the Puffin has only to stand on its cliff-top nesting site to present a rather comical appearance. The name 'sea parrot' is most appropriate, because the large, conical, colourful bill makes the bird look a little like a South American macaw. Most of the breeding colonies are on inaccessible islands or confined to grassy slopes some way down cliff faces, for the Puffin is a hole nester. On off-shore islands with grassy tops, particularly if they are colonized by rabbits, Puffins nest in burrows, and the sight of birds popping in and out of holes in the ground adds to the their amusing image. Towards the end of June, when the birds are feeding young, arriving birds carry beaksful of small fishes, all carefully laid across the bill. Somehow the bird manages to catch more fishes while still holding the first ones caught. The actual size of a Puffin colony is extremely difficult to assess, for the numbers that can be seen from day to day vary considerably and seem to bear no relationship to the numbers of occupied burrows. The daily pattern at the colony also varies but birds tend to congregate just off-shore in large rafts in the late afternoon before making the mass flight shorewards. Unfortunately, these behaviour patterns increase the difficulty in assessing population levels.

30cm

Ring Ouzel
Turdus torquatus

Here is a bird of the high ground, the mountain and moorland which always hold a more limited bird population than the lusher lowland sites. Among the Wheatears *(Oenanthe oenanthe)* and Meadow Pipits, this summer-visiting thrush adds its harsh 'chacking' call note and rich fluty song. This is the upland replacement for the more familiar Blackbird *(T. merula)*, from which it differs in having a distinctly scaly, rather grey plumage with very pale edges to the feathers and a prominent white crescent mark on the breast. Partially albino Blackbirds are often mistaken for this species although only extremely rarely do they possess all of the Ring Ouzel's characters. In June, young from the second brood are being fed in the nest which is usually placed on or near the ground in some convenient rocky cavity often in the side of a partly vegetated slope cut into the hillside many years before by an upland stream. The nest itself is rather like that of a Blackbird but it is bigger, bulkier, and much less tidy. The usual brood is four. With the fledging of the second brood, the upland areas are soon deserted, but not before the autumn berries that abound on the rowan trees and bilberry bushes are exploited to the full. Once the autumn migration is under way, Ring Ouzels can be encountered at almost any site, and they are often seen with flocks of other thrushes at coastal migration stations in the south-east.

24cm

Spotted Flycatcher
Muscicapa striata

An observer looking at an adult Spotted Flycatcher on its breeding ground might be forgiven for asking the question, 'Why spotted?' When the young emerge from the nest at the end of June, however, the question is answered for they are extremely spotted! Like all birds that feed predominantly on aerial insects, this species must leave Britain in the winter months to spend them in the southern regions of Africa. The Spotted Flycatcher is a rather late-arriving spring visitor. It feeds in the same way as most other flycatchers, sallying forth to snap up flying insects, from a prominent perch on a gate, a fence, or a low branch of a tree where it sits in typical upright posture watching carefully. Frequently, the bird returns to the same perch from which it started. Most of the insects taken are quite small but occasionally larger butterflies are pursued with vigour although, in most cases, the bird ends up with a beakful of butterfly wing rather than the insect itself. Apart from on the northern islands, this species can be encountered throughout the country. It often chooses to nest close to human habitations in larger gardens or parks where nest boxes with open fronts will frequently be occupied or where climbing plants attached to walls provide a perfect sheltered site for the nest.

14cm

Red-backed Shrike   *Lanius collurio*

The Red-backed Shrike has been declining as a British breeding bird for more than 100 years. Recently, it has been lost to many southern counties, at one time a stronghold of the species, with the only remaining concentrations in the coastal brecklands of East Anglia. The only hopeful indicator for the future of the species is that there are signs of some colonization in Scotland, presumably from the Scandinavian population, and a pattern is developing which resembles that for the Wryneck in that the bird is disappearing from the south and recolonizing the north. Shrikes on their breeding grounds have a characteristic food-storing habit whereby large insects, small birds, and small mammals are impaled on thorn bushes or barbed-wire fences from which they can be retrieved later. These food stores are known as larders and this behaviour is the origin of the name 'butcher bird' which was known to many people before the general decline of the species. The completed clutch of five or six eggs is usually in the nest by early June, and the same traditional site is often used year after year. The rather large nest is built by the male 1 to 2 metres from the ground and in a thick clump or hedgerow. It is often well hidden but its presence is indicated by the adult bird sitting prominently on the tops of nearby bushes.

17cm

Corn Bunting   *Miliaria calandra*

The Corn Bunting is one of the latest-nesting resident finches and does not begin laying until early June. The male, however, may well have been on the territory for several months continually singing the jingling song that is always likened to the shaking of a bunch of keys. Very much a bird associated with arable farmland, but absent from the high grounds of the north, west, and Ireland, the distribution is patchy and the bird's appearance is very erratic from year to year. The presence of rough, scrubby areas for nesting, particularly gorse, as well as prominent, isolated trees or overhead wires for song posts all seem necessary for the successful colonization of an area. There are numerous examples on record of polygamy in the species, the highest recorded incidence being one male with seven females, but this is probably exceptional and most males have only a single mate. Polygamy can take place because the females undertake virtually all of the breeding activities including nest building and incubation. She is not fed on the nest but leaves to feed, when she may be accompanied by the male. Young are also fed exclusively by the female with occasional assistance from the male. In some areas the species is double brooded and, very occasionally, the busy female manages to rear three broods.

18cm

JULY

The cereal crops in the open fields are turning yellow, and are even a golden hue when the sun is shining. The farm buildings are being deserted by the House Sparrows, the breeding season is coming to an end, although late broods of young are still chirping away from huge untidy nests tucked behind the guttering, under the eaves, or where a brick is missing from the barn wall. Collections of grass, straw, and string in the hawthorn hedge show where they attempted to nest away from the buildings but, although they are closely related to the weaver birds of Africa, they no longer retain the ability to build a tidy nest. The young from the earlier broods, together with the adults that have finished nesting, are now out among the golden corn fields where the flocks cling to the ripening ears, attempting, not very successfully, to extract the seed. Where the recent summer thunderstorm, with the sudden, unexpected downpour of heavy rain, has flattened some of the crop, they are having better success and are joined by small parties of Wood Pigeons and Mallard. Both species are normally prepared to wait until the crop has been harvested and perhaps the stubble burned before moving on to the fields to feed on the spilled grain, but the flattened stalks are too good an opportunity to miss. Each evening the Sparrows depart from the fields, heading for the local wood where a vast communal roost has been established and the many young finches congregate in the relative safety of the thick cover, much to the delight of the dusk-hunting Sparrowhawk or the nocturnal Tawny Owl. Out on the grazing meadows the young Lapwings have successfully fledged, the eggs having survived the passing of the bullocks' hooves and the occasional tractor wheel; the camouflaged young escaped the sharp eyes of the hunting Kestrel and Stoat until, eventually, the first tentative flight was undertaken. Now the flight feathers are fully grown, and the scattered broods have come together on the wet meadows where they have been joined by many early arriving Continental birds. Scattered among the Lapwings are several young thrushes and Blackbirds, all exploiting the abundant food supply in the soft ground.

Cormorant
Phalacrocorax carbo

Shag
P. aristotelis

These two closely related species have remarkably similar breeding distributions around the British coast. Both are absent in the south-east between the Humber and the Solent and, for both, the distribution on the north-east coast is patchy. But here the similarity in their breeding ceases, for the Shag is strictly coastal and rarely appears inland, while the Cormorant occasionally nests in trees at inland sites. Cormorants are ledge-nesting birds, usually in easily visible sites on cliffs or islands. Their nests are used year after year and their presence is marked by the extensive accumulation of droppings. Shags occupy less obvious sites, such as small, level crevices, or they may even conceal their nests among rocks and boulders or in small caves. The Shag is certainly the smaller of the two birds, and has a thinner bill with a more marked forehead. The plumage appears to be all black but, in fact, it is a dark bottle green and in summer, the Shag carries a small, tufted crest that turns forward on its head. The larger, blacker Cormorant shows white on the face and, in summer also has a white thigh patch. Because the Cormorant is the larger of the two, its flight is heavier and more ponderous, with slower wing beats. A further guideline to help separate the two species is the flight behaviour; Shags usually keep very close to the surface of the water while Cormorants will often fly at height. The birds exploit different food sources although both are fish eaters. The Cormorant is more a bird of the shallow waters, the diet consisting principally of the bottom-feeding flatfishes; whereas the Shag prefers to feed in deeper waters, diving and chasing free-swimming fishes. Because of this marked difference in the feeding behaviour of the two species, the Shags are able to inhabit rather more sites, and Cormorants always seek sheltered, shallow bays. Shags remain coastal throughout the year but, during the winter months, many Cormorants penetrate inland sites following river valleys to settle at suitable gravel pits or reservoirs where there is enough food to take them through the winter. A number of these sites can be in the centre of Britain, many kilometres from the coast. In the early spring the birds return to their coastal nesting areas, but, each year, some non-breeding immatures remain to summer. Those Cormorants with white under parts and that appear on the local reservoirs in July are the non-breeding, summering birds.

88cm

76cm

Greylag Goose

Anser anser

Historically, the Greylag was a native British Goose; the only goose to remain and breed following the departure of the winter flocks of other species. Nesting populations existed as far south as Lincolnshire but a decline in numbers and a contraction of the bird's range took place as land improvements, drainage, and intensification of agriculture all took their toll. The native population retained a rather tenuous hold in the Highlands of Scotland and in the western isles, with the present-day, wild breeding stock centred near the national nature reserve at Loch Druidibeg, Uist (OS map 22). With the development of artifical water areas throughout Britain as a result of increasing gravel extraction, construction of water-storage reservoirs, and so on, conditions were suitable again for recolonization by the species. In the past twenty-five years there has been an increase in the number of ornamental waterfowl collections throughout Britain as well as a growth in the conservation activities of the then Wildfowlers Association of Great Britain and Ireland which have led to a distribution of potential breeding birds to many sites from Kent to Northern Ireland. Birds always prefer to nest on islands where they are safe from human disturbance and from potential ground predators such as foxes. In July the pairs have young and the sight of both adults accompanying a brood of goslings is now a common occurrence in places like Kent, East Anglia, the Lake District, and south-west Scotland.

85cm

Canada Goose

Branta canadensis

In July Canada Geese are in moult so they are flightless. This large and familiar waterfowl, now to be seen on so many lakes and ponds throughout the country, has an interesting history. It originates from North America, and the entire British breeding population is the result of escapes and deliberate introductions either as ornamental waterfowl or as genuine attempts to aid the birds' colonization in the country. In its native North America the Canada Goose occurs in a range of sizes depending on the geographical area. Virtually all the British stock is descended from the larger forms. Very occasionally, at west-coast localities such as the Hebrides or Isles of Scilly, apparently genuine transatlantic vagrants occur. These can be distinguished by their size because they are far smaller than any of the races normally found in Britain. It is known that Charles II kept Canada Geese in his collection in the late 1600s and, in 1731, the first escaped bird was recorded and shot on the Thames. From this date onwards the numbers and range have steadily increased as more and more birds were released and, as flocks built up, young and flightless moulting adults were caught and transported elsewhere. By 1940 the species had achieved recognition as an official 'British bird' but they have never become the huntsman's quarry to the extent that they have in North America.

90cm

Buzzard

Buteo buteo

52cm

The Buzzard is very much a bird of the north and west but, surprisingly, it is absent from most of Ireland except the extreme north coast. In July, the bulky nest contains young. It is built in a wide range of sites from the tops of trees to suitable rocky crags or sea cliffs and is constructed largely from branches and twigs. The traditional sites are added to year after year until the structure may be as much as 1·5 metres in diameter. The number of eggs in a clutch varies from two to as many as six, but the latter is unusual. The wide-ranging clutch size is a response to available food supply. The more readily the adults can feed, the more eggs they are likely to lay and the more young they are able to rear. In extremely poor food years some adults will not attempt to breed at all. The Buzzard will eat a wide variety of food and, although it will catch and kill living prey, it is also a scavenger and searches for suitable corpses. Where rabbits are abundant, they undoubtedly form the bulk of the diet, as well as keeping the vegetation cropped to enable the birds to catch smaller prey such as voles or mice. The birds show three distinct methods of feeding: firstly, by soaring and searching in vulture fashion so that they can see other Buzzards descending upon a suitable carcass; secondly by perching on some prominent post or tree waiting to drop on passing prey; and thirdly by picking up small food items such as large beetles on the ground.

Lapwing

Vanellus vanellus

30cm

The breeding cycle has been completed, the Lapwings are flocking. Pastures and meadows, particularly the lower-lying sites, are attracting large flocks and, in areas like West Sedgemoor, Somerset (OS map 193), the flocks can run into many thousands of individuals. Not only do these accumulations include the British breeding stock, but also large numbers of Continental visitors are involved. From late May onwards a marked arrival of Lapwings takes place in south-east England. Many of the early birds must be failed breeders or non-breeders. The numbers increase during June and, in areas such as the open farmland of Romney Marsh (OS map 189), a high proportion of the flocks will be of non-British stock. There are few species more widespread in Britain. Any open country with short vegetation, particularly farmland, will suffice and the presence of birds is immediately obvious because of their striking black-and-white plumage and distinctive 'pee-wit' call which gives the bird one of its many alternative names. Severe winters certainly have a serious affect upon the feeding possibilities for the species and high mortality takes place in some years, frequently coupled with a marked southerly movement to warmer climates. Counts carried out in recent years, however, indicate that the total British breeding population is in excess of 200 000 pairs.

Curlew

Numenius arquata

July, and the Curlews are changing their habitat. They spent the summer on their breeding grounds on the moors, heaths, bogs, and meadows, but then the birds move back to their wintering sites on the coastal mudflats and estuaries where they become communal after their solitary life-style during the summer. Virtually every British estuary holds a population of Curlews from late July onwards, but the largest numbers at this time have been recorded at Morecambe Bay, Lancashire (OS map 97) where as many 16 000 birds have been reported. Numbers decrease as the winter progresses and the birds move further south and out of the country, but they increase again with the return passage in the spring. The Curlew is the largest British wader, weighing up to 1000 grams or a little more, and measuring some 55 to 60 centimetres from tip of bill to tip of tail (about 15 centimetres is the length of the very long, down-curved bill). Just as the habitat changes with the seasons, so does the feeding technique. On the breeding grounds the bird uses its bill much more for picking from the surface and tentatively probing among the vegetation. In winter the soft mud of the estuary is probed to the full length of the bill to reach worms and shellfish which cannot be exploited by any of the other mud-feeding waders.

61cm

Green Sandpiper

Tringa ochropus

Very occasionally a Green Sandpiper will summer in Britain, and nesting has been recorded in extremely rare circumstances in the north, but birds more often winter in Britain, particularly in the south. Otherwise this is a passage migrant, a bird which moves through Britain each spring and autumn on its way between the wintering grounds in south Europe and AFrica as far as the Equator, and its breeding grounds in northern Europe, particularly Scandinavia. The first of the autumn's returning birds will appear in July. These are probably unsuccessful breeders because the short northern summer still prevails. Any small muddy pool, marsh, ditch, or farmyard pond will provide a home for this freshwater wader that avoids the coast. Usually solitary, when disturbed it flies off with a fluting whistle, climbing and twisting in the air rather like a Snipe. The plumage appears to be all dark except for the contrasting white rump. The only bird with which it might be confused is the Wood Sandpiper *(T. glareola)* which is only slightly smaller and also has a white rump. The Green Sandpiper is darker, with dark underwings compared with the whitish grey of the Wood Sandpiper. Green Sandpipers' feet do not project beyond the tail in flight, the legs are green rather than yellow, and the upper parts are less speckled.

33cm

Redshank

Tringa totanus

In July, the Redshanks have young and they are incredibly noisy. They yelp out a warning if any danger threatens their territory, a warning that is heeded by virtually every animal that lives in the marshes, wet meadows, or other damp nesting areas. The adult birds will sit in a prominent position, such as the top of a fence or gate, piping away in full view while the young remain hidden in the vegetation. Only when the danger is past does silence return and the adults bring out their young with soft calls which encourage them to emerge into the open to feed. There are records of Redshanks moving their young to more secure situations by carrying them between their thighs, which is more usually associated with Woodcocks *(Scolopax rusticola)*. It is doubtful if this technique would be used for long distances, but certainly over a relatively short move, such as clearing a river or a wall, it serves a useful function. Far commoner as a breeding bird in the north than in the south, the Redshank has a particularly patchy distribution in Wales, Ireland, and the south-west. By late July, however, the breeding season is finished and the birds begin the return journey to their coastal wintering grounds. Few British breeders leave the country and large congregations assemble in the estuaries and on the mudflats; their numbers swollen by Continental immigrants.

28cm

Spotted Redshank

Tringa erythropus

Unlike its close relative the Redshank, Spotted Redshanks breed from northern Scandinavia eastwards and most only pass through Britain on passage, although small numbers do remain during the winter months and a few non-breeding birds summer here. In July the return autumn passage is under way and many of the birds retain their striking plumage of speckled black on the upper parts and under parts. This is in sharp contrast to the winter plumage when the birds are considerably paler with white below and grey above. Although Spotted Redshanks may often be found at inland freshwater sites, they concentrate at the coastal localities; the south-east holds the biggest numbers and the peaks occur in the Medway and Swale estuaries, Kent (OS map 178). The bird differs from the commoner Redshank in having longer legs and a longer and much finer bill. Spotted Redshanks make use of their longer bills by feeding in deeper water, wading belly deep or even swimming while still probing the mud by submerging bill, head, and neck. In flight the bird lacks the white trailing edge that occurs on the wings of the Redshank, but retains the whitish tail and rump, the white extending up its back in a V shape. The distinctive 'shu-wic' flight call readily indicates the presence of the species.

30cm

Herring Gull

Larus argentatus

Not very many years ago, the Herring Gull was the 'seagull', confined as a breeding bird to the sea cliffs and coastal islands around the British coast. Thanks to man and the ability of the Gull to be highly adaptable, this has now changed and large numbers can be encountered virtually anywhere at any time. Nesting is still mainly coastal, but Herring Gulls may also be found exploiting the flat tops of islands, buildings including factories and private houses, or even open beaches in less disturbed sites. The birds are now also prospecting buildings inland, and pairs have even nested in parks in central London. Increasingly, non-breeding individuals (and the species takes four years to reach breeding maturity) and wintering adults move inland for their food supplies, finding items to supplement their diet on the rubbish dumps, playing fields, and gravel pits. Generally, however, they will eat anything and they have even been reported to cannibalize their own young. They make the most of the waste provided by modern-living man. Most birds, however, gather around the harbours and docks or scavenge the tide-line, where a common feeding behaviour is to drop shellfish in an attempt to open them and get at the fleshy contents. A close look at the winter Gulls, however, shows them to be spending the majority of their day resting in flocks on some suitable meadow or on rocks, a clear sign that food is easily located and prolonged feeding sessions are unnecessary.

61cm

Little Gull

Larus minutus

In the late 1960s and early 1970s, the Little Gull was increasing as a visitor to Britain, with reports of larger and larger parties summering here. Many were subadults, but among them were a few in full adult plumage and, in several places, display and nest building were observed. Indeed, at the RSPB reserve at Fairburn, Yorkshire (OS map 105) nesting was attempted but the eggs were eaten. In more recent years the species has returned to being a less numerous visitor and most of the the birds are, once again, in immature plumage although their distribution is very widespread both inland and coastal. This small gull is rather tern-like in its flight, fluttering over the water either hawking insects or picking food items from the surface. The short, rounded wings are completely black beneath and white above in the adult, while the immatures show dark diagonal lines on the upper surfaces that meet on the body to present a w shape. An adult in full summer plumage has a completely black hood.

28cm

Kittiwake

Rissa tridactyla

Compared with the majority of the gulls to be seen in British waters, the Kittiwake exhibits a distinctly gentle appearance, lacking the rather wicked or vicious look of most of our gulls. Extremely rare inland, this highly marine species is only found regularly on shore during the breeding season when it resorts to steep cliffs and rocky islands off Britain's north and west coast. The most favoured localities are shared with Guillemots and Razorbills in vast numbers, and the birds are packed in side by side in rows along the natural ledges on the cliff-faces. In July, the young are steadily growing in the nest and the colony is at its noisiest with the ringing cries of the adults giving the bird its name – 'kittie-waak'. The young birds are most distinctive with a black bar across the nape, diagonal black band on the wing, and a black terminal band on the tail. The rather uniform pale-grey plumage of the adult contrasts strongly with the jet-black, triangular-shaped mark on the wing tips which suggests to many that the wings have been dipped into a bottle of black ink. The Kittiwake population has been steadily increasing for many years and new nest sites continue to be colonized. The species is spreading southwards on the east coast of England where, in addition to the natural cliff-ledge nests, birds are now breeding on man-made buildings in such places as Newcastle and Lowestoft.

41cm

Wood Pigeon

Columba palumbus

For a bird which lays only two eggs in a very flimsy nest, the Wood Pigeon is a remarkably successful species. The hand of agricultural man has been turned against the bird for many years because it learnt to exploit the cereal crops, fields of green vegetables, and subsequently the suburban garden. It is now to be found in very urban localities, even walking the London parks and squares in company with the more familiar 'London pigeon'. The Wood Pigeon is classed as a 'pest', so that large numbers are shot and nests are regularly torn from the trees, but the population remains large. Although July is the peak of the Pigeon breeding season, and all the coppices and woods seem to be filled with nests, the species will breed throughout the year. Very often a clutch of eggs may be laid before the young from the previous clutch are independent of the adults. Few birds are less attractive than a recently hatched Pigeon; the large, soft bill, generally naked appearance, and the lack of co-ordination of neck and head movements give the chick a rather reptilian look. When they are not breeding Wood Pigeons form large flocks which descend upon any suitable food supply where they behave communally, moving around en masse and eventually congregating in large roosting assemblies that can number many thousands of individuals.

41cm

Cuckoo

Cuculus canorus

Of all the birds that are resident in Britain or, are visitors, the Cuckoo probably has the most familiar call. Its voice, together with the arrival of the first Swallow, are widely thought to mark the true beginning of spring. Cuckoos are not here for long, however, and many of the adults have left the breeding grounds and assembled at southerly localities ready to leave Britain. Adult Cuckoos are among the first summer visitors to depart because, with no parental responsibility, there is no reason to stay. Once they are independent of their foster parents, young birds may remain until late September. In July, the adult birds exploit a food source that is neglected by virtually every other bird. The Cuckoo is able to eat hairy caterpillars. In years and in areas that these caterpillars reach plague proportions, it is possible to come across 'flocks' of Cuckoos all enjoying a rare feast that would otherwise be ignored. At the same time that mature Cuckoos are leaving Britain, many young birds are spilling over the sides of the foster nests as their foster parents, tiny by comparison, try to satisfy the voracious appetite and fill the ever-open gape. Foster parents vary but the most common are Dunnock *(Prunella modularis),* Meadow Pipit and Reed Warbler, and young female Cuckoos reared by any of these species are more likely to lay their eggs in the nest of that species.

33cm

Robin

Erithacus rubecula

If the Cuckoo is the British bird with the most familiar voice, the Robin is probably the most familiar sight. Although it is widespread throughout much of Europe and Asia, it is only in Britain that the Robin has become so tame and has become associated with gardens and parks. Robins can be extremely pugnacious towards their own kind, defending their territories against all intruders and sometimes even resorting to physical fighting, a rare event in the bird world. Some individuals become so tame, however, that they will take food from the hand and will even enter houses in search of food or to find a suitable nest site on a shelf or on the top of a cupboard. The familiar warm brown plumage with red breast that extends upwards to include the face and forehead is present on both sexes throughout the year, except on the young birds as they leave the nest. In July, later broods are fledging, for, particularly in southern Britain, Robins may rear three broods in a season, and it is these young that are the only Robins not to have red breasts. In the nest, the first plumage replaces the downy covering which Robins have shortly after hatching. This plumage is a well-speckled brown throughout, ideal camouflage for a bird trying to be inconspicuous in the bottom of a nest. Within two weeks of leaving the nest, the young Robin begins a body moult and, at the same time, the bird acquires the red breast.

14cm

Crossbill
Loxia curvirostra and L. scotica

The Crossbill is a rather unusual finch and has developed many fascinating aspects to its life history. This is a bird of the coniferous forest, for the special adaptation of crossed mandibles has evolved to enable the bird to open and extract the seeds from coniferous cones. The bill may cross in either direction and each seems to be equally effective for extracting seeds. The males have bright-red plumage with contrasting dark wings, while the females and young are green or yellowish with prominent streaking. This is an early nesting species, often starting in February, and, in most years, the season has been completed by July and family parties are present in the woods. After a successful nesting season a one-way migration will take place because of high population density following breeding. The birds will disperse generally westwards in search of new sites and, in many cases, they will not move back but remain to breed and thus colonize a new area. One result of this migratory behaviour is a rather patchwork distribution that can change from year to year; in England, however, such general areas as the Kielder Forest, Northumberland; the Brecks, Norfolk; the New Forest, Hampshire; and Forest of Dean, Gloucestershire, all hold permanent populations. North of the border, the Scottish Crossbill is now considered to be a separate species. Although the Scottish Crossbill is slightly bigger and has a stronger bill than the spruce-feeding Common Crossbill, it is extremely difficult to separate the two species on appearance alone.

16·5cm

House Sparrow
Passer domesticus

There can be few birds more closely associated with man than the House Sparrow. It has been spread throughout the world, and has steadily adapted its life-style to fit in with man's changing habits. As a breeding species in Britain it is only absent from some of the highest mountainous areas of northern Scotland; otherwise it may be encountered throughout the country and various estimates suggest a total breeding population in excess of five million pairs. In July, with the completion of the main breeding season, vast flocks of House Sparrows gather in rural areas. They also feed on the cereal crops before harvest time so they are regarded as agricultural pests. The species suffers a very high mortality in all habitats; the domestic cat takes a large toll and the House Sparrow is one of the commonest species to be killed on the roads. Formerly large numbers were trapped and killed by man, but little attempt is now made to control the species although it is still classed as 'pest'. The large population is maintained by an extended breeding season for, if the weather is mild, House Sparrows will continue breeding throughout the year.

15cm

AUGUST

The height of the holiday season, and the sandy beaches are filled with families who have travelled from their inland homes to seek temporary relaxation at the seaside. On the river estuaries, where the sand is replaced by mud – thick, black, and clinging – the human holidaymakers are absent but, within this rich sediment, washed down over the centuries by the rivers, is an abundance of small animal life that can provide food for the probing, thrusting bills of countless waders. The British breeding Curlews have deserted their moorland nesting sites and are back on the estuarine wintering areas, adding their distinctive cries to the voices of the returning species from the high arctic nesting grounds. The arctic summer is very short and, by early August, the season is complete and the birds must start their return journey. Grey and Ringed Plovers are back on the edges of the muddy areas. These two species have short, stout bills more appropriate for picking from the surface or among the weeds and stones than probing into the deep mud. Among the larger probing Curlews are the Redshank, Dunlin and Godwit while, out on the open mud, are the fully grown broods of Shelduck, dabbling, sitting, and grazing for food items left stranded by the retreating tide. This is an area where the tides control and govern all activities; the daily comings and goings follow a six-hour cycle, as the exposed mud reveals a massive food source. Two short months earlier, on the rocky crags a few kilometres along the coast, a brood of Peregrines had successfully fledged and the young are now independent of their parents. For the first time they have found it necessary to kill their own food. Two of the birds have discovered the undisturbed but bird-rich area of the open estuary and, at intervals throughout the day, a high-soaring Peregrine appears from its distant roosting site back on the crags and disturbs the feeding flocks of waders. As they take flight, the Peregrine's wings are folded back along its body and the bird goes into a steep, fast, and powerful dive. An individual prey item is selected, perhaps just a little less active than the others in the flock or slightly incapacitated by an old injury, but with a small puff of feathers it is struck down and the Peregrine makes a successful kill.

Black-necked Grebe *Podiceps nigricollis*

August is not a favoured month for visiting the reservoirs and gravel pits of central and southern Britain in the hope of seeing water birds. The great concentrations of wintering wildfowl have yet to arrive. By the middle of the month, however, the rather scattered populations of Black-necked Grebes in Europe will be on the move. In Britain only small numbers of the birds breed in lowland Scotland so that it is presumably the unsuccessful or non-breeding birds that are the first to appear on the southern stretches of water. It is not easy to separate this species from the Slavonian Grebe *(P. auritus)* when they are both in winter plumage, and even experienced birdwatchers may argue over a bird as they peer through their telescopes. But the time of year can help because the more numerous Black-neck will be present from late July, peaking in mid–August, while the less common Slavonian Grebe rarely appears before late September. To confirm the identification, look for the Black-neck's uptilted tip to the bill, the black on the crown extending below the eye, and the generally dusky appearance of the cheeks and neck. The Slavonian appears to be a cleaner, more black-and-white individual. Any area of open water, often inland, is worth checking but the reservoirs and gravel pits of west London (OS map 176) have always been favoured sites.

30cm

Garganey *Anas querquedula*

Unique among the British ducks in that it is a summer visitor, the Garganey spends the winter in Africa and appears each year at scattered sites, particularly in the east of England. Garganey arrive in early spring and the first birds appear in late March. It is often one of the earliest of all the summer visitors and arrives well before the last of the huge numbers of wintering wildfowl have departed. In July the males are starting to lose their distinctive breeding plumage with the broad white stripe curling backwards from the eye to the nape and the blue-grey forewing that is so obvious in flight. By August the males will be very similar to the females and, eventually, all the birds flock, frequently mixing with Teal and easily overlooked because of their similar size. One of the strongholds of the species is the fenlands of Cambridgeshire (OS map 143), but nowhere are they common. The male has a unique rattling call which is unlike the call of any duck, but it is highly distinctive. The Garganey is able to produce this call because the physical structure of its windpipe is different from that of other ducks.

38cm

Ruddy Duck
Oxyura jamaicensis

The Ruddy Duck is a relatively recent addition to the list of British birds. It is a late-breeding species and many are still on eggs during early August, when they inhabit areas of open water with shallow, well-vegetated margins where many of the nests are on floating reed platforms. The population is steadily increasing but some of the largest concentrations of breeding and post-breeding birds are to be found on the meres and lakes of Cheshire (OS maps 117 and 118). The history of this species as a British breeding bird makes a fascinating story. It is a North American duck that was unknown in the wild in Britain until the 1950s, when breeding pairs were imported to the Wildfowl Trust at Slimbridge, Gloucestershire (OS map 162), and, subsequently, young were reared which remained free winged. By the early 1960s nearly 100 young Ruddy Duck had flown from Slimbridge, and breeding on nearby reservoirs was taking place. From these early birds are descended the British population which has bred at such widely spaced areas as Lough Neagh in Northern Ireland, Loch of Kinnordy in Scotland, and recently colonized sites in the south and east. In 1971 the Ruddy Duck received the honour of being added to the official list of British birds because it had satisfied the criterion of having a self-supporting wild population.

40cm

Shelduck
Tadorna tadorna

Very much a coastal duck, the Shelduck is found wherever tidal mud provides access to its staple diet of marine molluscs. In recent years, however, the bird has tended more and more to nest inland although, as yet, this is still very much confined to the river valley systems, particularly these of the Humber and Ouse on the east coast. The Shelduck may be thought of as a link between the ducks and the geese, and, unlike many ducks, it chooses to nest inside holes or buildings, or under haystacks, where the distinctive black-and-white plumage does not immediately disclose the position of the nest. Both sexes are similar in plumage and, as do the geese, both parents attend the young after hatching. July is the season of the moult migration when the vast majority moves out of Britain heading for the Heligoland Bight off the German coast, where the birds become flightless as they renew their plumage. At this time the young birds, still not capable of flight, are herded together into a creche, often consisting of many broods, where they are looked after by a small number of adults which do not leave for the German moulting grounds.

60cm

Peregrine

Falco peregrinus

In August the young Peregrines are on the wing, and hunting birds can be encountered on many of the sea-cliffs in the west and north of Britain. This is a bird with a chequered history since the control measures were introduced during World War II to protect pigeons carrying vital messages. Populations have risen and then fallen again; the Peregrine Falcon suffered a serious decline when the use of agricultural pesticides was at its height and, not only did birds die, but their breeding success was seriously affected because the egg shells became thinner and were easily broken in the nest. The range contracted, most of the breeding pairs on the east and south coast were lost, and a serious decline was observed in the west. Only in the northern coastal areas and Highlands of Scotland did the Peregrine maintain its numbers, for, in these parts, it was well clear of the arable farmland where the chemicals were most widely used. Voluntary control and bans on the use of chemicals resulted in a slow but notable recovery in the population from the early 1970s, and, although Peregrines have still not returned to some of the traditional sites in the east, many of the western areas have now been repopulated. August is a good month during which to see the Peregrines hanging on the wind high above the sea-cliffs waiting for a passing pigeon.

45cm

Ringed Plover

Charadrius hiaticula

As a breeding bird, the Ringed Plover is widely distributed around the coast of Britain, favouring the sandy or shingle beaches for nesting where, unfortunately, it is very vulnerable to disturbance from the holidaying public. There is an increasing tendency, however, for breeding birds to colonize inland sites, following the river valleys, and, in some areas, exploiting the gravel extraction industry which provides artificial beaches. By mid-August the autumn flocking is taking place and most of the birds are back on the coast – the western estuaries where mud gives way to the upper sand are most favoured. As the month draws to a close the autumn migrants from Iceland and Greenland, on their way to the African breeding grounds, pass across the Irish Sea and marked concentrations are recorded on the estuaries of the Severn (OS maps 171 and 172), the Dee (OS map 117), and Morecambe Bay (OS map 97). Following the departure of these passage migrants, the British breeding stock remains for the winter, and studies of ringed birds show that the estimated British breeding population of some 6000 pairs, mainly concentrated in the east and north, moves to the Irish Sea for the winter months. Indeed, the birds which nest along the East Anglian coast travel across the country to the favoured western sites. At most times of the year the estuaries of Britain hold an internationally important population of this species.

19cm

Grey Plover

Pluvialus squatarola

A true passage migrant and winter visitor, the Grey Plover does not nest in Britain, but moves south from the high Arctic to winter over a wide area of the northern and southern hemispheres. Then it becomes strictly a coastal bird and rarely concentrates in the dense flocks of its close relative the Golden Plover *(P. apricaria)*. During August the small numbers that arrived in late July are steadily augmented by further arrivals, numbers increasing to reach an eventual peak in early September after which the passage birds move further south to leave the British wintering stock. Detailed studies of this species indicate that there is a marked pattern to the arrivals. The first to appear, in late July and early August, are the immature birds that are too young to breed but have returned to the northern nesting grounds for the summer. These are closely followed by the breeding adults, many of which still retain traces of the summer plumage which is so characteristic of this species in the spring migrations. Finally, the birds that hatched that year, with their boldly spotted yellow plumage, start arriving from the end of August. Most estuaries hold some birds; the largest concentrations are in the east and south with particularly high numbers on The Wash (OS maps 131 and 132) and Chichester Harbour (OS maps 196 and 197).

28cm

Greenshank

Tringa nebularia

In a year of high population, there may be as many as 1000 pairs of Greenshank nesting in northern Scotland. This is probably exceptional and the figure will be nearer 600 pairs in most years. Following their departure from these wet moorland breeding slopes, there is a southerly movement with the majority of the birds wintering in Africa, athough a few remain in some British coastal areas particularly in the south and west. August is the month of peak passage when Scandinavian birds pass through on what is very much an overland migration. Also, any area of water such as a pond, gravel pit, sewage farm, or reservoir can attract the passing migrant bird, and it is not unusual in this month to flush individuals or small parties from most unlikely places. Occasionally, these migrant birds are encountered temporarily intermingled with flocks of other waders but, more often, they are solitary or keep to their own species. The distinctive triple call 'chu-chu-chu' is so easily recognizable once it is known that birds can be heard calling as they pass over the most unlikely areas on their nocturnal migration through central England. Further west, and particularly in Ireland, the autumn passage peak takes place in September, several weeks after the peak movement in the eastern areas.

30cm

Red-necked Phalarope

Phalaropus lobatus

The Red-necked Phalarope is an extremely rare breeding bird on the islands of northern Scotland and coastal Ireland where it is often associated with old peat diggings. It also occurs as a scarce passage migrant in Britain and, in August, individuals may appear at a wide variety of wetland sites particularly on the east and south coast where they have arrived after being blown off course from the Scandinavian migration route. It is a remarkable little wader and shows very little fear of man, often allowing a very close approach. Indeed, on the breeding grounds there are records of birds continuing to brood young which are being held in the hand. The feet are lobed, rather than webbed and, although the bird will feed by wading, picking from the mud and surface of the water with its fine, needle-like bill, it also employs a specialized 'spinning' feeding action. The swimming bird spins rapidly on the surface of the water causing a disturbance which brings food items to the surface that can be easily picked up.

18cm

Stone Curlew

Burhinus oedicnemus

A national decline of the breeding population in the 1970s has severely restricted this species to a very few sites in southern England. Although the striking vocal display of the bird has ceased by August, the far-carrying flight calls can still be heard. Some pairs may still be rearing young from late broods which are probably from replacement clutches. The Stone Curlew is a nocturnal bird and is highly crepuscular in its activities so it is best to look for it in the late evening. By late August, the family parties have grouped together to form post-breeding flocks before they depart on their southward migration. Evening visits to the open country of East Anglia and Salisbury Plain, or perhaps the southern downs, may provide exciting sights and sounds, especially if you couple the visit with a search for another nocturnal species still vocal at this time, the Nightjar *(Caprimulgus europaeus)*. A favourite spot is the Norfolk Naturalists' Trust reserve at Weeting, Norfolk (OS map 143).

41cm

Common Tern

Sterna hirundo

Most of the British breeding Common Terns occur at coastal sites although smaller, scattered colonies are found at a variety of inland localities, usually on secure islands in lochs or reservoirs. Increasingly, however, the species is exploiting the network of gravel pits now available. By August the birds have returned to the coast and the autumn migration is under way, many following the English coast on their way south to the west African wintering grounds. Prominent headlands such as Spurn Point, Humberside (OS map 113) or Dungeness, Kent (OS map 189) are popular seawatching points where the movements of these and other seabirds can be observed. If the weather, and particularly the wind, is suitable and there is a light onshore breeze, their numbers can be large and the movement will continue throughout the day. Many of the Common Terns are in parties mixed with other species and it is often difficult to separate them from the closely related Arctic Tern. In those birds that are still in full summer plumage, there is a number of features which will help to distinguish the two species: the black tip to the crimson bill of the Common Tern compared with the all-blood-red bill of the Arctic; the very translucent appearance of the Arctic Tern's wing when viewed against the light; indeed, the whole appearance is very pale compared with the much greyer wing of the Common. When seen side by side in flight the Arctic Tern looks as though it has a longer tail and this effect is enhanced because its wings are set further forward.

35cm

Little Owl

Athene noctua

The Little Owl is not a native British species but it is now to be found throughout most of England and Wales and small numbers are nesting in southern Scotland. It is very much a bird of open farmland and it is often active during daylight hours sitting prominently on the top of a fence post or corner of a farm building. Small woods and coppices will be occupied if they do not already contain pairs of the more typical woodland species, the Tawny Owl. The first attempt at introducing Little Owls into Britain occurred in 1842 when some were released in Yorkshire but were never seen again. In the late 1880s several releases, totalling some forty birds, took place in Kent and from there they bred successfully and spread into Sussex and Surrey. Following subsequent releases in Northamptonshire and Hertfordshire, the Little Owl had arrived. At various times during its spread and colonization, the species has received much adverse publicity concerning its diet. Therefore, a very detailed study of the bird's food was undertaken, including examination of nest contents, stomach analysis, and a detailed look at the undigested food pellets regurgitated by this and all the birds of prey. About half the diet consists of insects and the other half small mammals and birds.

22cm

Swift

Apus apus

One of the latest of the summer migrants to arrive, the Swift is among the earliest to depart and only a small proportion of the summer population remains after the end of August. A truly avian species, the feet and legs have become reduced to mere hooks which enable the bird to hang on a rough surface, and they certainly do not allow the bird to stand. To leave its nest site within the eaves of a house or a church tower, the bird simply uses its wings to drag itself to the edge of the nest from where it falls into flight. If it becomes grounded because of abnormal weather, the Swift can only get into the air again if it is on relatively open ground and there is some wind to assist takeoff. The flying ability of swifts is legendary, and an Asiatic species has been credited with being the fastest flying bird in the world. Our Swift feeds, mates, collects nest material, drinks, and sleeps on the wing; and so important is its flying insect food supply that it will travel large distances to avoid major cyclonic weather patterns where food is absent. Fine days with southerly winds on the south coast of England in August will often prompt a marked passage of Swifts, leaving for their African wintering grounds.

16·5cm

Wryneck

Jynx torquilla

Once a common breeding bird in the south-east of England, with a stronghold in Kent, there is now only a small nesting population in Scotland, and it is only likely to be encountered as a wind-displaced migrant on Britain's east coast. With easterly weather over the North Sea area, migrants travelling south in Scandinavia can find themselves blown out over the sea to make landfall in Britain anywhere between Shetland and Sussex. The latter half of August and early September are the most likely to provide the best chances to see the bird, and birdwatchers looking for this species as well as for other east-coast vagrants, such as Bluethroats *(Luscinia svecica)* and Icterine Warblers *(Hippolais icterina),* should watch the weather maps for an easterly wind coupled with overnight rain in southern Scandinavia. Ideally, too, there should be a rather dull, cloudy start to the day on the English coast. If all looks well, a visit to an east-coast promontory, such as the observatories at Spurn, Humberside (OS map 113) or Dungeness, Kent (OS map 189) could well prove rewarding. It should be immediately obvious if the chances are high because large numbers of Pied Flycatchers and Redstarts are good indicator species that Scandinavian birds are present. On a really 'big' day, the numbers could run into thousands of birds and, with careful searching, Wrynecks should be found among them.

16·5cm

Chough

Pyrrhocorax pyrrhocorax

A bird of the western sea-cliffs, the Chough has declined considerably in recent years because of the changes in farming technique that have taken place on the cliff-top feeding areas. Historically, it occurred along the south coast from Kent to Cornwall, and Cornwall has a particularly close association with the species which is often known as the 'Cornish Chough'. The present stronghold of the bird is in western Ireland where it is particularly abundant on some of the south-west sea-cliffs, and on the Isle of Man, and in Wales. Inland pairs occur in some mountainous areas. The distinctive decurved red bill and red legs contrasting with the all-black plumage make this a particularly striking member of the crow family, and, unlike other members of the group, the Chough has more pleasing habits. It is not a scavenging or carrion-feeding bird but uses the pointed, down-curved bill to dig out insects from soft coastal soils or from the drying dung of grazing cattle. By August the breeding season has been completed and the family parties have combined to form foraging flocks that can consist of as many as five or six different broods. These flocks will often 'play' along the cliff faces, tumbling and twisting in the rising air currents, gaining height only to plummet downwards on half-closed wings.

39cm

Dunnock

Prunella modularis

The Dunnock is probably one of the most overlooked but most widespread of all British birds. It is only absent as a breeding species from the Shetlands and from some of the highest mountains in Scotland. Predominantly a ground-feeding bird, it moves from cover with a rather mouse-like shuffling gait, the streaked brown plumage and grey head adding to its inconspicuousness. When disturbed Dunnocks will flight quietly into cover and 'disappear'. Even the bird's song is rather easy to miss, and may perhaps be mistaken for a rather brief burst from a Wren or a slightly faster song from a Robin. Overlooked they may be, but they are everywhere and quietly exploit almost every habitat available from mature woodland to town park and garden and open heath and moorland. The Dunnock used to be known as the 'Hedge Sparrow', a singularly unsuitable name because it has no relationship with sparrows. Hedge Accentor would have been more accurate but perhaps it is rather a clumsy name and so, gradually, Dunnock became accepted and preferred to the many alternatives. Each county appears to have developed its own country name for this species, ranging from 'Shuffle-wing' in Surrey to 'Blue Jig' in Scotland.

14·5cm

Yellow Wagtail

Motacilla flava

The Yellow Wagtail is very much associated with water, particularly the wet meadows, river valleys, and reclaimed marshes where the water-filled dykes are numerous. As a summer visitor and breeding species, the bird is virtually confined to England and, even there, it is absent from the far north and south-west. In August the breeding season is past, the birds are completing their post-breeding moult early in the month, and the family parties combine to form feeding flocks that exploit the abundant insect population that is present until well into September. Then the Wagtails depart for their African wintering grounds. During the month, any grazing meadow, complete with cattle and water, will provide a feeding site for the Yellow Wagtail. The adult males are particularly striking and bright compared with the duller females and immatures. The cattle help the birds to feed by disturbing insects, and the Wagtails can be seen running between their feet and snapping up their quarry – and it is not just the ground-living insects that are claimed. The back of a cow or horse provides a convenient perch from which to fly up and intercept any passing flying insect to provide a meal. As dusk approaches, the Wagtails depart to occupy a communal roost, often in a reed bed and shared with the resident Pied Wagtails.

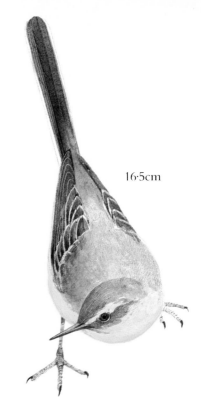

16·5cm

Linnet

Carduelis cannabina

August, and the Linnets have deserted their breeding grounds on the heaths and open areas where gorse and bramble provide such excellent nest sites. The birds are flocking for the winter months and it is 'all-change' among the British Linnets. Birds which have bred in Britain move southwards, crossing the English Channel, often in mixed flocks with Goldfinches, to spend the winter months in the milder climate of Iberia. Meanwhile, back in England their place has been taken by individuals from further north and east which, also accompanied by Goldfinches, have crossed the North Sea to spend the winter on the open saltmarshes and farmlands of Britain. It is somewhat surprising that the Linnet should be one of the more regular of the less frequent hosts for the Cuckoo because the diet is completely unsuitable. It would appear that when the nest of the preferred host is not available, a Linnet's nest is an acceptable alternative. But, of course, the young Cuckoo is bound to die because the diet of seeds is valueless to a bird that requires large quantities of insects. The autumn flocks were once a favourite target for the bird trappers, as the Linnet has always been a popular cagebird, an excellent songster, and a species that would regularly hybridize with the canary. Nowadays the only legal trapping is carried out for the study of migration, the birds being released with a ring and allowed to continue their journey.

13cm

SEPTEMBER

The woods have now accepted the quietness that followed the song-filled months earlier in the year. The huge numbers of young birds, reared and fledged on the abundant caterpillar food supply that literally dripped from the oak trees, have now largely departed. Only the late straggler remains among the warblers and flycatchers that return each spring to exploit this seasonal abundance. The dense vegetation that provided such a secure moulting area is now starting to lose its bright green as the leaves begin to take on the autumn's yellows and browns. Among this dying-back of the woodland habitat, there appears a rich food supply of seeds and fruits. The insects may be in decline but, on the edge of the oakwood, the thick bramble patches are heavy with blackberries and very few birds can resist such a feast, for the high sugar content is readily converted to energy. This is particularly important for the migrants which are preparing for a journey that will take them south of the Sahara. Deeper in the wood different species are turning to different food sources. The Bullfinches are eyeing the ash tree keys as they slowly ripen, hanging in thick clusters. The squirrels are attacking the hazel nuts, while the fallen nuts are nibbled by the wood mice and others are carried off to be carefully opened by deft blows from the bills of Nuthatches or Green Woodpeckers. The abundance of any particular seed crop varies from year to year, often governed by the weather in the preceding season. In years when acorns are extra numerous, the whole pattern of bird life in the oakwood can change. Wood Pigeons no longer need to fly off to the local farmland in search of a suitable crop to decimate, and the farmers talk of a lack of Pigeons. Instead, they need hardly leave their woodland roost, for the floor of the oakwood is littered with acorns, and the Pigeons' crops are rapidly filled so that the birds can spend the remainder of the day sitting around slowly digesting the meal. The Jays become extra active, flying around carrying acorns, storing them away for future use by pushing them into the soft autumn soil. Many are retrieved later in the year but just as many are never recovered and a small number eventually germinate and grow to ensure the future of the oakwood.

Manx Shearwater   *Puffinus puffinus*

The scientific name of the Manx Shearwater was not acquired as a result of mistaken identity but because, when it was first named, the label was used to indicate that this Shearwater shared its island nesting burrows with those of the Puffin. Traditional nesting sites are used year after year, and they are all on the north or west coasts, but the nocturnal habits of the bird mean that estimating the total population is extremely difficult. However, perhaps half-a-million nesting pairs would be a reasonable guess. By September the breeding colonies have been deserted and the birds have become strictly marine only to be seen from coastal headlands after strong winds or far out to sea from boats. The long-distance movements and homing ability of the species have become legendary. British breeding birds regularly move to and from the Bay of Biscay while wintering individuals often occur off the Atlantic coast of South America. Indeed, at least one bird must have rounded the Horn because a dead individual bearing a British ring has been washed up on the Australian coastline. Experiments with marked birds have shown that they have an astonishing ability to return to the breeding grounds even if they are released in an area that is never normally visited by the species. Individuals from the Welsh colony at Skokholm Island have successfully returned from North America and Venice. In the case of the latter it is not known if this was by an ocean route through the Straits of Gibraltar or by a direct overland flight.

35cm

Mallard   *Anas platyrhynchos*

The Mallard is the commonest and most familiar of all the British ducks, inhabiting almost every wetland site from the smallest pond to the largest lake or reservoir. In urban situations it becomes extremely tame, accepting food from the hand and nesting in exposed and very obvious situations. In a more rural setting the Mallard distrusts man because of the annual shooting season which begins in September, and the presence of natural predators, including foxes and crows, means that the species is far more secretive. Nests are well hidden and even sites high up in trees are used. The British breeding population is estimated at some 40 000 pairs with influxes of winter visitors from northern and eastern Europe raising this total to over 350 000 individuals in the depths of the winter. These high numbers reflect the general adaptability of the species, for its food ranges from insects and water plants to grain collected on the stubble fields and artificial foods supplied by man. Mallard tend to move towards the coast during the autumn and to remain there for the winter in places where the water does not freeze. The contrast between Mallard occupying the quiet waters of a park pond in central London and those withstanding the buffeting gales off the Northumberland coast is quite striking, but they belong to the same species.

58cm

Mute Swan

Cygnus olor

Like the Mallard, the Mute Swan needs no introduction as a British bird. The well-established pairs on ponds and rivers remain in the same site year after year and are a familiar part of the scenery. Herds of non-breeding individuals are generally more wary and are likely to settle where they can graze and will crop either grass or shooting cereal plants. The origins of the Swan in Britain have been the subject of much debate. Some authors credit its arrival, along with the fallow deer and the Pheasant, to the Romans; while others are inclined to suggest it was introduced by Richard I. Whatever its origin, and it is also possible that it was a wild indigenous species in Britain, it is certain that formerly the bulk of the population was kept in captivity in a semidomesticated state. Over a period of time the birds were left to go wild or to escape from the moats and lakes of their owners and thus colonize the country as wild birds. With such a large and familiar bird it is possible to assess the breeding population and results suggest a figure of some 6000 breeding pairs plus about 12 000 non-breeding birds.

150cm

Kestrel

Falco tinnunculus

Often mistakenly called a 'Sparrowhawk' this is the falcon that feeds by hovering. Hanging almost motionless in the air or, if the conditions are calm, on rapidly beating wings, the bird is searching the ground below for suitable food items ranging from small mammals or young birds to beetles and earthworms. As the Kestrel hovers, the long tail is used to stabilize the position of the body, adjusting for the slightest change in wind speed and direction and enabling the bird to keep its head absolutely motionless as it uses its keen eyesight to watch for the slightest movement below. A possible prey is located and the bird loses height rapidly, then stops and hovers nearer the ground as if to check that everything is as it should be before the final plummet earthwards. The prey is usually eaten where it is trapped or, if it is too large to be dealt with immediately, it is carried off to a regular feeding site known as a 'plucking post'. Ever the opportunist, the Kestrel saves hovering energy by hunting in a similar fashion but watches from the top of a conveniently placed telephone pole or electricity pylon. The national network of motorways has given the species rich feeding areas for the short-cropped grass embankments provide just the right kind of terrain for this method of hunting. A motorway journey is rarely completed without the sight of a few Kestrels.

35cm

Red-legged Partridge   *Alectoris rufa*

A native of southern Europe, the Red-legged Partridge was introduced into Britain in the late 1700s by those seeking to increase the variety of gamebirds present. Although introduction attempts were made in various parts of the country, the East Anglian releases were the most successful for here the light, sandy and stony ground must have most closely resembled their home habitat. Introductions continued and, although breeding now takes place as far north as Scotland, the south-east of England, and particularly the fens and brecks of East Anglia remain the stronghold. Following the recent decline in the Grey Partridge *(Perdix perdix)* population, game-rearing establishments have concentrated even more on the Red-leg and have, in addition, taken to rearing the Chukar *(A. chukar)* and Rock Partridge *(A. graeca)*, closely related species from south-east Europe. Many of these are now well established and freely hybridize with the Red-legged Partridge so that the British population is developing into very mixed stock. A bigger and heavier bird than the Grey Partridge, the Red-legged or French Partridge is less inclined to fly when disturbed and more likely to run. In September, the winter coveys, usually consisting of one or two family parties have assembled in the open countryside and favour the farmland and heaths where the striking black-and-white face pattern and boldy streaked flanks are very obvious.

35cm

Partridge   *Perdix perdix*

Although it has always been absent from Highland Scotland and western Wales, the Grey Partridge has been suffering a slow and steady decline in numbers since the 1950s. This decline was noted even earlier in Ireland where the species is now extremely scarce. Attempts at artificial rearing and releasing have not halted the decline and, although the bird is still widespread, its numbers are now low. This steady decline can apparently be attributed to a variety of factors which include: an increasing tendency for cold wet springs to seriously affect the food supply; the appearance of agricultural chemicals, including herbicides, which remove much of the feeding cover needed by the young; and changing farming techniques which remove many of the hedges, burn the stubble, and plough in the autumn. The large areas of cereal fields are not suitable for the Partridge which is a bird of mixed arable and pastoral feeding where the fields are interspersed with hedges that provide the secure nesting sites. The September coveys are never mixed with the Red-legged Partridge and, unlike that species, the Grey or English Partridge is likely to explode into flight when disturbed displaying the similarly rufous tail but lacking the black-and-white face markings.

30cm

Wood Sandpiper *Tringa glareola*

There are small numbers of breeding Wood Sandpipers located in northern Scotland but the population is extremely low and it is as a passage migrant that the bird is best known in Britain. The main movement is recorded in the autumn months in south-east England, although numbers vary from year to year. They occasionally appear in small flocks but they are usually seen as individuals. Inland records can be as frequent as coastal reports, and the birds may choose to stop at almost any small wetland area from a muddy field or village pond to reservoirs or gravel pits. The Wood Sandpiper is very much a bird of freshwater and, in coastal sites, they are more likely to be encountered behind the sea wall on the dykes and ditches rather than on the open tidal mud. The more numerous Green Sandpiper is the only species with which the Wood Sandpiper is likely to be confused because both birds show prominent white rumps when flushed. The Wood Sandpiper is less black and white, however, and has speckled upper parts and a pale underwing. The pale stripe over the eye is always apparent and the rather long, yellowish-green legs protrude beyond the tail in flight. When flushed the bird gives a highly distinctive 'chiff-chiff-chiff' flight call which is strikingly different from the more whistling flight note of the Green Sandpiper.

20cm

Common Sandpiper *Actitis hypoleucos*

Having deserted the breeding grounds on the upland rivers and lakes of northern Britain where they nest beside the fast-flowing streams and quiet, still waters where stony beaches have been created to provide suitable feeding areas, the Common Sandpipers depart on their autumn migration. Very occasionally birds will overwinter but the majority moves south with many passing into Africa. The British passage birds have their numbers swollen, particularly in the east, by the Scandinavian birds that have crossed the North Sea. During late August to mid-September coastal freshwater areas in south-east England will often hold considerable concentrations. Kent, as the extreme south-east corner of the country, is a particularly favoured area and it is the Stour estuary at Sandwich Bay (OS map 179) that appears to attract the largest numbers with more than 100 often noted and, on one occasion, a massive total of 300 individuals. More frequently the Common Sandpiper is encountered as a solitary individual and, when disturbed, it flies off with a trilling flight call, low over the water's surface in a characteristically flicking flight action that is interspersed with glides on downward-bowed wings.

20cm

Little Stint *Calidris minuta*

Stints are the smallest of the waders and, at first glance, they are rather like small Dunlins *(C. alpina)* with which they frequently associate. On closer examination, however, there are numerous differences that, once seen, make this a distinctive species. Occasional birds winter or occur in Britain in spring but principally the Little Stint is an autumn passage migrant, numbers varying greatly from year to year as the species moves from its northern Russian breeding grounds to the winter quarters from the Mediterranean southwards. Indeed, the Little Stint is credited with being one of the long-distance migrants, individuals from the arctic breeding grounds reaching South Africa. Passage birds exploit most wetland habitats but are more frequent on coastal pools in the east although inland records and small parties in the west are not unusual in peak years. Compared with the Dunlin, the Little Stint is smaller, and has a short bill and short legs which serve to distinguish it. The feeding action is rapid and, unlike the probing of the larger species, the Stint more often picks food items from the surface. Most birds seen in Britain each autumn are young ones that appear very pale; the upper parts are a rich buff coloration with prominent pale fringes to the feathers that form a characteristic v mark on the back.

13cm

Curlew Sandpiper *Calidris ferruginea*

The appearance and movements of the Curlew Sandpiper through Britain closely resemble those of the Little Stint, for this is another high-arctic nesting species that passes through Britain on migration to its Mediterranean and tropical wintering grounds. It is scarce at all times of the year apart from in the autumn when numbers vary greatly. In some years massive influxes occur and in others the bird is extremely scarce. This is apparently a reflection of the general weather pattern over much of western Europe, and bears little relationship to the general population levels. Most of the birds appear in September on the east coast and numbers venturing inland are generally small. In peak years many birds seem to arrive in the north-east, after which some travel over land to migrate southwards through the Irish Sea, while other follow the east-coast route. Slightly larger than the closely related Dunlin, the Curlew Sandpiper has longer legs on which it frequently wades up to its belly when feeding, a longer, finer, slightly decurved bill, and in winter plumage, a prominent pale stripe over the eye, a distinctive flush on the breast of the young birds, and, in flight, the most distinctive characteristic of all, a prominent white rump.

19cm

Black Tern

Chlidonias niger

Although it is not a British breeding species, the Black Tern is a regular passage migrant, particularly in the south and east where peak numbers are to be found in late August and early September. It is a frequent inland visitor to reservoirs and gravel pits, but the largest numbers are still to be found at coastal sites and, on migration, they will readily follow the coastline in company with the 'sea terns'. Black Terns, however, are generally known as 'marsh terns' because of where they locate their breeding sites. When feeding the birds behave socially, the small parties 'hawking' over some small stretch of water until, as if by a pre-arranged signal, they will move on. They do not dive for food but hover and flutter over the surface of the water, dipping down to snatch up some food item, especially recently hatched insects. There are records of Black Terns 'hawking' for insects in a Swallow-like fashion over dry ground. In autumn the birds can display a bewildering variety of plumages as the adults moult from their dark, smoky grey summer dress with the blacker body, into the grey and white of winter. The juvenile birds are different again, being very dark and mottled on the upper surface of the wings and back, but, in common with the winter-plumaged adults, they have a white collar and dark shoulder mark.

22·5cm

Stock Dove

Columba oenas

The Stock Dove is a common species and is on the increase in Britain. It has spread from its stronghold in south-east England to colonize the entire country except for northernmost Scotland. In the late 1950s a rather sudden and sharp decline in the numbers of Doves in the east is attributed to the use of toxic chemicals but, since then, a recovery has taken place and this species is numerous once again. Very much a bird of farmland, it often associates with Wood Pigeons outside the breeding season when the behaviour of the two species is more similar. Generally, Stock Doves are outnumbered by their larger relatives, but the two will readily share the same roosting site after they have exploited the same food supply throughout the day. Usually, however, the movement between these two points is undertaken in separate flocks. The RSPB reserve at Northward Hill, Kent (OS map 178) regularly holds a sizeable roost of both species and a peak count of some 8000 individuals shows that the Stock Dove was outnumbered by two to one. Slightly smaller than the Wood Pigeon, this species lacks white on the wings and neck and, in flight, shows shorter, more rounded wings with faster wing beats.

33cm

Green Woodpecker
Picus viridis

In common with all woodpeckers, the Green Woodpecker is absent from Ireland and, only in recent years, has it spread northwards to colonize northern England, and from the early 1950s, southern Scotland. The northward spread continues and it has been calculated that this is taking place at a rate of nearly 10 kilometres per year. This is the largest of the British woodpeckers. It is not a bird of true woodland and prefers more open areas such as parkland and large gardens which contain mature trees so that there are suitable nesting sites and open ground upon which the species regularly feeds. It has a particular liking for ants. The Green Woodpecker is a very noisy bird with its ringing, laughing cry that is known as the 'yaffling' call. This explains the origin of one of its local names, the 'Yaffle'. Country legend has it that the species is particularly vocal before rain so that it has been given the names 'Rainbird' or 'Rainfowl' in counties as far apart as Sussex and Northumberland. The large size and distinctive green-and-yellow coloration make this an unmistakable bird as it flies across open country with deep undulations – a wing flap and then forward dipping progress on closed wings followed by another wing flap. The unwary birdwatcher in the south-east should be cautious about attaching the label, Golden Oriole *(Oriolus oriolus)* to a bright-yellow bird.

33cm

Jay
Garrulus glandarius

Basically a resident species, this brightly coloured member of the crow family is very much associated with woodland and is absent from the more open areas of upland and marshland Britain. England and Wales are the strongholds of the Jay while the geographically distinct subspecies is slowly spreading through Ireland no doubt because of the increased tree planting that is taking place. Over the years the Jay has suffered considerable persecution at the hands of man and, in most areas, it is a shy, retiring bird that is most frequently located by its harsh cry. If it is seen at all it is usually only a retreating white rump disappearing among the foliage. Many surburban areas have now been colonized, however, and, since the 1930s, the birds have moved to the central London parks where a breeding population is now well established. Here the birds are no longer wary and they will readily accept food from the public. There are two features of the Jay's annual cycle which are very evident in September. Acorns, the staple diet of the species, are gathered in the oakwoods and secreted away by burying for later use. Many of these are never recovered and germinate to produce young oak trees. In years of high population levels continental Jays may undertake migratory invasions and large numbers can appear in south-east England. In 1957, for example, nearly 1000 Jays were recorded arriving in Essex on one day in September.

34cm

Wheatear

Oenanthe oenanthe

The Wheatear is one of the earliest of the summer migrants to arrive back on its British breeding grounds. It not only uses the remoter, more upland areas of Britain as its nesting sites but also makes use of the British Isles as a giant stepping stone on its spring and autumn migrations. The breeding range of the species is large, spreading from Alaska westwards through Asia and Europe to Greenland and north-east Canada. Virtually all the birds winter in Africa and long-distance migration is undertaken annually. The breeding birds from Canada, Greenland, and Iceland pass through the British Isles, particularly Ireland and the Irish Sea region each autumn, the largest numbers in September after the local breeding birds have all departed. Observations made at sea suggest that some birds cross direct from Iceland to Spain, but most hop from island to island to reach their destination. Obliged to make this extensive journey twice a year, these so-called 'Greenland Wheatears' have developed into larger, brighter birds with a more upright stance than the British breeding examples. The further north the Wheatears travel the larger they become; those of Iceland are bigger than those from Shetland and bigger still are those from Greenland, and so on.

15cm

Whinchat

Saxicola rubetra

September is the month in which to find the migrating Whinchats on Britain's east coast. They drift across the North Sea at times of easterly winds and, together with other Scandinavian night migrants, their arrival is frequently recorded at bird observatories such as Fair Isle, Shetland (OS map 4) or Spurn Point, Humberside (OS map 113). At this time the British breeding stock has left the nesting areas and, although concentrations are most likely to be encountered at coastal sites, many birds are recorded at inland localities where the species favours open farmland and exploits fences and buildings as convenient perches from which to watch for food items on the ground below. Whinchats are essentially insectivorous, feeding largely on beetles and caterpillars although they eat spiders, too, which are also picked up from the ground. Many flies are captured in a typical fly-catching manner by short flights in pursuit of passing insects. It is possible to confuse the Whinchat with the closely related Stonechat *(S. torquata)* in immature autumn plumage because the two species are similar in size and shape and both indulge in fence perching. The Whinchat is paler, mostly sandy coloured with a streaked back, and it has a broader pale stripe over the eye. As it flies from the prominent perch the distinctive white basal sides to the tail are visible.

12·5cm

127

Firecrest

Regulus ignicapillus

Similar in size, shape, behaviour, and voice to the Goldcrest *(R. regulus)*, this equally small bird is best distinguished by the broad white stripe over the eye, bronze-coloured area on the shoulder, and slightly darker back. The voice can be distinctive, but the difference is subtle, requiring either a very good ear for sound or considerable familiarity with the species. The song is slightly deeper in tone and lacks the final flourish that is such a feature of the song of the Goldcrest, while the call is harsher and can include a very Robin-like 'tick' note. Although small numbers have been discovered nesting in southern England in recent years and a wintering population regularly occurs in several southern counties, particularly on the Isles of Scilly (OS map 203), it is as an autumn passage migrant between its German breeding grounds and Spanish wintering quarters that it is most often recorded. Even then the appearances are very restricted and are usually concentrated at coastal sites between Essex and Sussex, with three localities, Sandwich Bay (OS map 179), Dungeness (OS map 189), and Beachy Head (OS map 199) providing the bulk of the records. Observers who have watched this species in many countries of the world have often expressed surprise at finding them on the Kent coast in flocks. The peak figure appears to be seventy birds at Dungeness on one day.

9cm

Bullfinch

Pyrrhula pyrrhula

From being a truly woodland species, the Bullfinch has adapted and changed to inhabit a wide variety of sites from gardens and parks to open farmland. As long as small coppices or tangled clumps of vegetation are available for nesting, the species can apparently survive. It is resident and migratory movements are virtually unknown which is probably why it has never managed to colonize the Scottish Highlands or the Isle of Man. It has been suggested that the increase in the numbers of Bullfinches is a direct result of the decline of the Sparrowhawk, for, being such a conspicuous bird, it would fall easy prey to such an efficient bird hunter. The behaviour and life history have been studied in great detail, because in some areas where fruit farming is a major industry, the economic implications of a bird with a strong liking for buds are obvious. Detailed fieldwork has shown that Bullfinches prefer seeds, particularly those of the ash trees, and in the autumn these form the staple diet. In poor years, however, when the seed supply is quickly exhausted, the birds look elsewhere for their food. Because of their encounters with many orchards, Bullfinches are no longer protected in many countries and have been extensively trapped. This seems to have temporarily alleviated the problem in particular areas but appears to have had no effect on the total population of Bullfinches.

15cm

OCTOBER

The view across the wide expanse of reed bed to distant wet meadows and the saltmarsh that leads to the open sea looks particularly birdless at this time of year. Small numbers of duck, largely Mallard, but including a few Teal and Shoveler, are mingled with the Coots on the open water areas among the reeds, while the site is shared with a small collection of Herring Gulls that have flown in from the shore to bathe in the sheltered lagoons. Having surveyed the area for some while, it is time to move on, but suddenly the waterfowl scurry to cover among the reeds with a great deal of splashing and noise. The disturbing factor, however, holds no real threat, for a lone Short-eared Owl, probably freshly arrived from its Scandinavian nesting area, is quartering the ground, more interested in an unsuspecting vole than a full-grown Mallard or Coot. As the Owl passes in front of the viewing position it, too, shows concern and makes a rapid change of direction because, from the opposite side of the reeds, a female Hen Harrier is similarly quartering the cover. Another recent arrival that will probably remain for the winter, the Harrier not only feeds in the area but, together with

several others of the same species, forms a communal roost deep within the reeds. The Owl and Harrier indulge in a mock aerial battle for just a few seconds, each bird twisting and turning and gaining height before they resume their individual hunt. Neither poses a threat to the other; it is almost as if they enjoyed the temporary break from the serious business of finding food. As they pass out of sight the scene returns to that of its original quietness; so typical of birdwatching where a sudden burst of activity and interest is followed by a spell of stillness. Beyond the reeds and over the wet meadows, another short burst of activity is taking place. The small flock of Meadow Pipits, that has been feeding undisturbed beside one of the drainage ditches, is suddenly put to flight by the rapid, dashing approach of a hunting Merlin. Another recently arrived winter visitor from northern Europe, the small falcon twists and turns in flight in close pursuit of the Pipit. This time the small bird is lucky; it finds shelter in a dense grass tussock and the Merlin flies off still hungry.

Pochard

Aythya ferina

Colonization by breeding Pochard began in the late 1800s and the species is now widespread but still local throughout the British Isles. There is a total population only slightly in excess of 200 pairs, mainly concentrated in the south-east with particularly high numbers on the Elmley reserve, Kent (OS map 178). During the autumn months a marked westward movement takes place as the birds desert the colder climate of eastern Europe, and the British wintering total reaches a maximum of 40 000 individuals scattered around the larger reservoirs and lakes of the entire country. At this time of year most Pochard are found on freshwater, but small flocks are often encountered on some of the estuaries and river mouths. Often associated with the closely related Tufted Duck, the Pochard is another of the diving ducks which spends its time either as part of a sleeping raft or in a compact feeding unit. The diet is varied, but it is mainly vegetable matter cropped from the underwater plants, although some aquatic animals are also taken perhaps incidentally. Dives will last for as long as 30 seconds and Pochard prefer a water depth of some 1·8 to 2·4 metres although food in shallower water is sometimes exploited. Occasionally, the birds will upend in the manner of a surface-feeding duck.

46cm

Hen Harrier

Circus cyaneus

By October the Hen Harrier has settled in to its winter distribution, favouring the low-lying coastal areas and open country, particularly in the south-east, although the Orkney Islands are probably the most northerly wintering grounds in the world for this species. The upland and moorland nesting sites have largely been deserted, remaining empty until the following spring, and Scandinavian birds have arrived to spend the winter in Britain while many of the British nesting birds have departed southwards. The open country favours the hunting technique. The birds quarter the ground with a seemingly slow, lazy flapping. They keep low and frequently follow a convenient bank or ditch, casually switching from side to side, ready to drop on to any suitable prey item which may include small mammals such as a field vole or an unwary feeding Skylark *(Alauda arvensis)*. Communal roosting is a regular habit of the species in winter, and reed beds, often with high water levels, are regularly used. The annual roost at the Stodmarsh National Nature Reserve, Kent (OS map 179) has become a well-observed event by birdwatchers. The hour before darkness can be an exciting time as the birds gather over the reeds, usually in a mixture of adult males with pale-grey plumage and the more numerous immatures and females in brown with a contrasting white rump.

45cm

Merlin
Falco columbarius

October is very much a month of Merlin migration. The
northern and upland breeding grounds have been deserted and
the movement is southwards or downwards so that low-lying
coastal areas are preferred to the bleak upland sites which,
throughout the winter, lack the small birds that form the staple
diet of the species. The total British breeding population is
probably less than 500 pairs and the evidence suggests that this
number is steadily falling. From October onwards, however, the
wintering population starts to arrive from two completely
different directions. The Icelandic birds follow a route via the
northern islands to winter in the west, throughout the Irish Sea
region, while the east-coast arrivals from Scandinavia are the
birds that will winter in the east and south. A Merlin hunting
over the open marshes is a spectacular site, with its dashing,
rapid, low-level flight guaranteed to flush a sitting Meadow Pipit
or Skylark, two of the favourite prey items. The aerial chase that
follows is one of twists and turns as the quarry attempts to
outmanoeuvre its pursuer, while the falcon seeks to follow every
movement and position itself above the small bird to enable it to
execute the final strike. Although it is a masterly flier, the Merlin
is far from 100 per cent successful in the hunt.

30cm

Jack Snipe
Lymnocryptes minimus

The Jack Snipe is a winter visitor to Britain and arrives from its
north European breeding grounds from September onwards.
The peak arrival occurs in October on the east coast from where
it spreads westwards throughout the British Isles. Numbers are
generally small, and the Jack Snipe is easily overlooked for,
unlike its larger relative the Snipe, it is not readily flushed, it is
usually silent, and rarely appears in flocks. It prefers a muddier
habitat than the Snipe does, often in areas where floodwater has
recently receded to leave dead or dying vegetation as suitable
camouflage. The cryptic coloration of the upper parts with its
metallic purple and green as well as the buff striping makes the
crouching bird almost invisible. It is necessary almost to step on a
Jack Snipe before it will take to the wing. With its rather weak,
direct flight action, the bird rarely flies far, but drops back into
the vegetation without a single sound being omitted. Observers
lucky enough to watch a feeding bird in the open will note the
rather bouncing gait whereby the bird moves as if it is attached to
springs at the top of its legs. When the Jack Snipe is actively
feeding the body remains still, the bird turns its head to probe the
mud around itself in a series of thrusts, and then moves on to the
next suitable feeding patch.

19cm

Woodcock

Scolopax rusticola

Unlike most waders, the Woodcock is a woodland species living and nesting among dense vegetation, in complete contrast to the normal open areas of mud and sand inhabited by the majority of wading birds. To survive in this situation the species has evolved several important features. The plumage has become patterned with brown and black, the perfect cryptic coloration to blend in with the dead leaves and dappled sunlight on the woodland floor. It is more important for the bird to be able to see upwards rather than forwards, because forward vision would be obscured by the vegetation, so that the Woodcock's eyes have become greatly enlarged and are set high on the sides of its head with the shape of the skull narrowing towards the crown. This gives the bird almost complete all-round vision, both upwards and backwards. To achieve this, however, the ear has had to move from the normal position behind the eye and is now situated below it. The extremely long bill has a very sensitive and pliable tip with which the bird is able to locate earthworms by probing into the soft ground beneath the covering of leaves and woodland litter. Each October, birds from Scandinavia and eastern Europe move westwards and arrive on the English east coast from where they disperse throughout Britain, travelling even further west and south in periods of cold weather but favouring any woodland site with suitable ground cover.

34cm

Dunlin

Calidris alpina

The Dunlin is the commonest and most familiar of the coastal waders, breeding in small numbers on some of the upland sites, mainly in the north, but a few pairs find their way as far south as Dartmoor. In winter, the bird becomes almost entirely coastal although small numbers may appear at inland localities on migration or in times of hard weather. Britain is situated at a 'crossroads' for the various populations of the species, with Scandinavian and Russian birds arriving to spend the winter here, while birds from Greenland and Iceland pass through on their way to the north-west African wintering grounds. At various times of the year, and particularly during the December to February period, many British estuaries are internationally important for the species, but, in autumn, the highest concentrations occur on The Wash (OS maps 131 and 132) which becomes a major moulting ground so that the numbers of passage birds are swollen by individuals remaining to complete their annual moult. All birds must undergo at least one complete moult each year because, to retain the powers of flight, it is obviously important that the plumage is kept in perfect condition. At such times the birds require safe feeding and resting areas, and the wide expanse of tidal mud that surrounds The Wash fulfils this function perfectly.

18cm

Mediterranean Gull

Larus melanocephalus

The Mediterranean Gull is an excellent example of a species for which the status has changed dramatically as observers have been better able to identify it. As a breeding bird it is very much confined to the eastern end of the Mediterranean and Black Sea coast and, when the once standard reference work, *The Handbook of British Birds* (Witherby, *et al*), was published in 1941 only ten records were known in Britain, of which six have been subsequently disallowed. By comparison, in the period 1958-67 more than 285 birds were recorded, and October marked the end of a four-month period when most were reported. The bird can now be regarded as an annual visitor to most coastal counties, but it still remains commonest in the south-east and breeding attempts have taken place within colonies of Black-headed Gulls, a feature which has also developed on the Continental mainland. It is extremely difficult to assess changes in this gull's numbers because of the increased awareness of observers, but the striking white appearance, with no black on the wing tips, means that the adult is particularly obvious and probably unlikely to be overlooked. The immatures, however, are more difficult to identify, closely resembling young Common Gulls but showing a more contrasting black-and-white appearance compared to the rather brown-and-grey markings of the commoner species.

39cm

Short-eared Owl

Asio flammeus

Although it is generally considered to be a diurnal species, the Short-eared Owl is most active at dusk and dawn and could more truly be described as crepuscular. It is not unusual, however, to encounter a hunting bird in daylight during the winter when immigrants from Scandinavia and eastern Europe have arrived in Britain to exploit the milder climate and feed on the voles that live in the rough pastures and saltmarshes. The numbers of this owl vary greatly from year to year for this is a particularly nomadic bird that follows its food supply. In years when voles are particularly plentiful large numbers of owls will remain but, when vole populations are low, the owls move on to search for food elsewhere. When hunting, the birds adopt a rather harrier-like method, quartering the ground on seemingly slow, casual wing beats, or in glides on wings held upwards in a shallow V. The flight, like that of all owls, is silent, and a hunting bird can easily drop on an unsuspecting prey. When not hunting, the Short-eared Owl usually chooses to roost in a tussock of coarse grass where it can settle into a position sheltered from the wind or from any rain. If these sites remain undisturbed, they will be used day after day and a heap of droppings and regurgitated pellets containing the indigestible parts of the most recent meal will steadily accumulate.

38cm

House Martin

Delichon urbica

The House Martin is a familiar summer species that has deserted its historical sites on the cliffs to exploit the man-made potential of the house. A member of the swallow family, it has pure-white under parts and a white rump which distinguish it from all the other species of the group. No-one knows why the birds choose to build their nests of mud beneath the eaves of any particular house for, in a row of apparently identical buildings, one always seems to be especially selected. As is so often the way of these things, the householders who would like the bird on their property are unlucky while those who have no wish to clear up the inevitable mess on the garden path have birds year after year. The House Martin is an aerial feeder, dependent upon flying insects for its food supply so that most birds have departed by October to escape the approaching cold weather. But each year, a surprising number of pairs attempts to rear just one extra late brood. Many of the established colonies will start the month with one or more nests still containing young and, occasionally, these will be fed not just by the parents but also by the young of earlier broods which sometimes return to the nests to roost. How successful these late broods are is unknown although certainly many of them fledge. Nor is it known whether or not these young birds are capable of the sustained flight to the African wintering grounds so late in the year.

13cm

Jackdaw

Corvus monedula

Generally considered to be a sedentary species, the Jackdaw is found throughout Britain except in northernmost Scotland. It inhabits a wide range of sites from coastal cliffs to buildings, farmland, and woodland. The Jackdaw is highly adaptable and is a great opportunist ready to exploit any suddenly available food supply. It scavenges the rubbish tips with the gulls, searches the tideline with the waders, feeds in the parks with the Starlings *(Sturnus vulgaris),* and joins communal roosts with the Rooks. Following independence from their parents, young Jackdaws may disperse over a distance of several hundred kilometres, but there seems to be no fixed pattern to this movement and it appears to lack direction. In October, however, a more definite migration reaches eastern England, and migrant birds from the low countries, often in company with Rooks and Hooded Crows, cross the southern North Sea to winter in the milder climate of the British Isles. These migrant birds tend to be slightly paler on the nape than the residents, but the differences are extremely difficult to see in the field. A familiar bird to man, the Jackdaw's name has been derived from its distinctive call, usually rendered as 'jaac' and, in situations where it is not threatened in any way, birds can become particularly tame and confiding.

33cm

Cetti's Warbler

Cettia cetti

A very recent colonist in Britain, the Cetti's Warbler's status has changed from that of an extremely rare vagrant to being a breeding bird occupying some twelve or more counties in the south-east with a total population well in excess of 150 pairs. All this has happened within fifteen years and the bird seems to be able to treat cold winter weather with indifference so that Britain has gained its second resident warbler. The centre of the colonization is still Kent, with a valley of the River Stour (OS map 179) holding the highest concentration. An examination of the story as it relates to Kent indicates just how rapidly the colonization took place. The first county record was that of a bird trapped at the Dungeness Bird Observatory (OS map 189) in 1968 with another there in 1971 as well as three at the Stodmarsh National Nature Reserve (OS map 179). Breeding was suspected in 1972 with the first confirmed British breeding record in 1973. By 1975, only two years later, more than sixty singing birds were in their territories and, by the early 1980s, some 100 pairs were resident in the county. The loud explosive song of this rather small, warm-brown, round-tailed warbler is the best indication of its presence in an area. Apart from during a short winter gap, the song can be heard throughout the year but the bird remains skulking and secretive so that most birdwatchers are unlikely to note the characteristic ten feathers in the tail as opposed to the normal twelve.

14cm

Willow Warbler

Phylloscopus trochilus

Commonest of the warblers to arrive and nest in Britain each spring, Willow Warblers have departed by early September. The bird's distinctive song, likened to the tinkling of notes running down the scales, can be heard briefly just before its departure but it will not be heard again in the British woodlands until the following April. October, however, usually holds some Willow Warbler surprises. The birds that breed in northern Europe are distinctly paler and larger than the British breeding birds; they lack much of the yellowness that is such a feature of our birds and appear to be a rather washed-out grey and white. They are different enough in appearance for the scientists to have given them their own subspecies name, *P.t. acredula*. They head for the African wintering quarters much later in the year normally taking a route that avoids Britain but, each autumn on October days with easterly winds, small numbers are displayed westward to make landfall on the English and Scottish east coasts where students of bird migration discover them among the incoming winter visitors and other Scandinavian drift migrants.

11cm

Meadow Pipit
Anthus pratensis

In common with all species of pipits, the Meadow Pipit is not easy to separate from its close relatives but, because it is the commonest of all the British pipits, it is the one most likely to be encountered. The plumage variation is considerable; those birds from western areas, including Ireland, tend to be reddish brown in colour, while the English and more eastern birds are more yellowish green and less boldly patterned. The most distinctive and consistent character is the call, a series of short notes which, once learnt, will serve to separate the Meadow Pipit from all others. On completion of the breeding cycle, many of the nesting areas are deserted, particularly the upland sites which prove to be inhospitable during the winter months. The birds move to lower altitudes where they inhabit farmland or the edges of reservoirs and gravel pits, while some move to the coastal saltmarshes. Many British breeding birds depart for the Mediterranean but others remain and their numbers are augmented by immigrant stock. When observing pipits the birdwatcher should note the streaking on the under parts which, on the Meadow Pipit should be small and dark but not black on a pale background; the legs are brownish or even slightly reddish tinged, and the outer tail feathers are white.

14·5cm

Rock Pipit
Anthus spinoletta

Larger, heavier, and greyer than the Meadow Pipit, the Rock Pipit has streaked blackish under parts on a dusky background, indistinctly streaked grey upper parts, darkish legs, and dusky outer tail feathers. It is very much a coastal species inhabiting the rocky coastline throughout Britain but moving in late autumn to inhabit the saltmarshes and open beaches of sites that are not suitable for nesting. Occasionally, Rock Pipits move well up river estuaries. Small numbers of Scandinavian birds arrive to augment this population. A separate geographical subspecies of the Rock Pipit, the Water Pipit *(A.s. spinoletta)* of central and southern Europe, migrates to Britain in small numbers each autumn to winter, not at the coastal sites, but at inland localities in southern England, favouring reservoirs, watercress beds, and similar sites. The call resembles that of the more familiar Rock Pipit, a single rather explosive note, but the bird is different in appearance. The upper parts of the Water Pipit are unmarked as are the rather pinky cream under parts in spring, but there is some fine streaking in winter. Its legs are dark and the outer tail feathers white. Most distinctive of all, the race has a rather clear grey head with prominent white stripes over the eyes.

16·5cm

Great Grey Shrike   *Lanius excubitor*

The Great Grey Shrike is one of the most widely distributed land birds in the northern hemisphere. It occurs across Europe, Asia, and North America, and southwards into North Africa, even inhabiting areas south of the Sahara. In fact, it is the only member of the shrike family to nest in four continents. In Britain, however, it is only a winter visitor in small numbers and then it is usually confined to the eastern half of the country. Many wintering sites are traditional, so that a bird may return to the same area for several years in succession and is apparently the same surviving individual. The favoured winter habitat is gorse-covered heaths with scrub and fringe woodland, but a wide variety of more open country may be selected. It is the largest of the European shrikes so that it will take quite large prey including birds the size of a Song Thrush *(Turdus philomelos)* as well as small mammals and large insects. The hunting habits are distinctive; the bird sits prominently on the top of a bush or fence post, showing its clear white breast to the full, and then it swoops downwards on any suitable prey. When changing perches, the bird drops almost to ground level, flying low over the vegetation and, at the last moment, it sweeps upwards to the new perch.

24cm

Greenfinch   *Carduelis chloris*

A widespread and familiar British breeding species, the Greenfinch welcomes October by beginning to return to suburban gardens where it exploits the readily available supply of food put out for wild birds. During the the late 1950s and early 1960s, feeding birds became almost an obsession for many people in several areas, particularly during very cold weather when commercially available wild-bird food was on sale in the high-street shops. One of the commonest feeding methods was to hang up string bags full of peanuts as food for the tits. Blue Tits *(Parus caeruleus)* and Great Tits *(P. major)* had already become accustomed to feeding on bacon rind and coconut so they quickly learned to take advantage of the new food source. The Greenfinch, too, soon learned how to feed from these bags and, more than most species, showed the necessary agility. Rather solitary during the summer months, by October Greenfinches are flocking, feeding and roosting communally, although roosts occupied on one night may be deserted the next. Dense stands of scrub such as holly and rhododendron provide the security necessary for an overnight roost and, at their peak, some sites can hold several hundred birds.

15cm

Chaffinch
Brambling

Fringilla coelebs

F. montifringilla

These two closely related species are remarkably similar in structure and habits, but the Chaffinch can be seen in Britain throughout the year while the Brambling is a winter visitor. The autumn finch migration can be seen in October and continuing through November. This is the time when large numbers of Continental finches move south and west to milder climates for the winter. Most of the birds move in single-species flocks but, among the Chaffinches is a scattering of Bramblings. The routes taken to reach Britain are very dependent upon the prevailing weather conditions, especially the direction and strength of the wind. If conditions are bad, the birds continue to follow the European coast and avoid crossing the open North Sea. Then they eventually make the short sea crossing over the English Channel, usually between the headlands of Cap Gris Nez on the French coast and Dungeness, Kent (OS map 189). If conditions are good for a North Sea crossing, the birds will make landfall on the East Anglian coast or, if the wind is blowing from the south, even further north. Many of the Chaffinches have divided into flocks of one sex, a common feature of winter finch flocks, but all give the distinctive 'chup' flight call typical of the species. Among these Chaffinch calls can be heard the harsh, nasal 'zeee' note of the Brambling. Flight calls are most important to the migrant flocks because they aid contact between the individuals and prevent the flock breaking up and becoming scattered. The Brambling differs from the more familiar Chaffinch in having orange rather than pink on the breast, and orange on the shoulders. It also has a darker back and an all-black tail lacking the white outer tail feathers. The Brambling's most distinctive feature in flight is the pure-white rump. One of the favourite food items of both species is beech mast, which is readily exploited in years when there is a good crop of seeds but, when this is not available, the woodlands are deserted and the birds resort to the open farmland, feeding on the stubble or weed fields. In cold weather, the finches will feed around the cattle or farm buildings. The Chaffinch is generally considered to be one of the commonest of all British birds with a nesting population of seven million pairs.

15cm

14·5cm

NOVEMBER

The overnight frost has lingered in isolated patches where the weak sunshine has not filtered through to warm the ground beneath the overhanging river bank. The autumn has been dry and the flow into the lake is sluggish and no competition for the small raft of waterfowl that swims upstream in advance of the birdwatcher walking along the bank. Throughout the summer the birds have grown accustomed to people, for this is a favourite walk but, by November, there are fewer visitors and the birds have regained a little of their wariness. Among the Mallards and Moorhens is the rather strange-looking Mandarin Duck, a species now well established as a wild bird following its escape from waterfowl collections. It has joined the Ruddy Duck, Canada, and Egyptian Geese as species of wildfowl that have successfully colonized Britain from introduced birds. As our birdwatcher continues the walk along the riverside path, a lone Grey Wagtail is flushed from the stony water's edge and, with its distinctive call and long tail, settles into one of the overhanging alder trees. This will be the Wagtail's winter base but, as the binoculars scan the tree tops, looking for the bird, it is not the Wagtail but a small yellow-and-green bird that is located, hanging from the alder catkins rather like a tit – a Siskin. A brief search of the canopy reveals a small mixed flock of Siskins and Redpolls working their way slowly through the trees, each bird quietly calling in its attempt not to lose contact with the main flock. As with the other birds, these will probably remain throughout the winter and a visit at any time during the coming months will find them again in the same area. Standing still, watching for a few minutes, the disturbance created by the birdwatcher's first approach subsides. With a loud, shrill call, a Kingfisher appears around the corner of the river, a brilliant flash of blue that settles on a dead branch low over the water. Through binoculars, the deep chestnut red of the under parts can be seen in contrast with the striking blue upper parts, but the fatal mistake has been made, a sudden movement with the binoculars. Another shrill cry and the Kingfisher is away, a dazzle of colour flying over the surface.

Storm Petrel

Hydrobates pelagicus

By November the isolated offshore nesting rocks and islands of the Storm Petrel have been deserted, and the birds have become truly marine. It is difficult to observe the species during the breeding season because it only comes to land during the hours of darkness and nests in holes and rocky fissures so that it is hidden throughout the daylight period. Watching from a boat is one way to observe the birds at sea but this is not always successful. The ability of such a small bird (only some 15 centimetres long, with a weight of only a little over 28 grams and a wing span of only 35·5 centimetres), to survive the autumn and winter in a completely maritime environment is quite astonishing. Indeed, some of the closest views of the birds are obtained in years when 'wrecks' occur. Under certain conditions, which always include strong winds, large numbers of Storm Petrels can find themselves blown out of their normal range to be set down on beaches or at inland sites. A late-autumn Storm Petrel 'hawking' over an inland reservoir is a most unexpected site and, of course, it is very unlikely that the bird would be able to return to sea. Under normal circumstances, the bird in its highly maritime habitat feeds from the surface of the water, fluttering with dangling feet just above the waves, appearing to be walking on the surface. This habit apparently resulted in the name 'petrel', originating from St Peter

15cm

Mandarin Duck

Aix galericulata

The Mandarin is perhaps one of the most striking and colourful of all the ducks. It is well known in Britain as a very popular member of ornamental waterfowl collections. Originating as a forest species in China and Japan, it was first imported into Britain in the mid-1700s. It was still very unusual, however, when the London Zoo bred the first British pair nearly 100 years later. Not long after that, in 1861 in Berkshire, the first escaped bird was recorded, unfortunately having been shot. By the 1900s free-living birds were being becoming established in many, often widely separated areas ranging from Woburn and Windsor Great Park to the River Tay in Scotland. Probably one of the best sites for seeing the species is at Virginia Water (OS map 176) and, in November, the males have shed their eclipsed plumage and grown the striking breeding plumage which allows such extravagant displays. By the end of the year the pairs will have been formed although the birds remain in flocks and small parties until late March and April when prospective nest sites, usually holes in trees, are examined and established.

43cm

Velvet Scoter

Melanitta fusca

A larger bird than the more familiar Common Scoter, the Velvet Scoter differs from it in several ways. The adult male shows white by the eye, yellow not orange on the bill, and has red rather than black legs and feet. The female has two prominent pale patches on the face, one in front of the eye and the other behind. At all ages and in all plumages the best identification feature is most obvious in flight: the pure-white secondary wing feathers, which contrast with the otherwise all-black plumage, can be seen even at a considerable distance and sometimes may even be apparent on the wing of a swimming bird. A winter visitor from Scandinavia and northern Russia, most of the birds have arrived by late November although further influxes will occur if extremely cold weather affects the southern Baltic. Most wintering birds can be seen on the north and east coasts and, although only about 1000 occur in comparison with the 20 000 wintering Common Scoters, they appear to be able to survive in rougher and more exposed seas. The larger size enables them to dive to a much greater depth – 20 metres as opposed to the Common Scoter's 10 – and for periods of as much as three minutes rather than less than a minute.

55cm

Rough-legged Buzzard

Buteo lagopus

November on the East Anglian coast, and it is a Rough-legged Buzzard autumn. Individuals have been seen arriving from out at sea in small numbers between Yorkshire and Sussex from early October but now the movement is at its height. Just why they should come in any one year and not another is not fully understood but probably reflects weather patterns, population levels, and available food supplies. Several individuals of this magnificent raptor in the air at the same time make a sight worth seeing, and the south Suffolk coast (OS map 156) can now boast this species in most winters. It differs from the Buzzard in having a white tail with a black terminal band, white under parts with a prominent black belly patch, and patches on the carpal joints of the wings. The hunting technique is also different from that of the Buzzard for the Rough-leg hovers while searching for food. It is a rather ponderous, heavy hovering, lacking the neatness and efficiency of the Kestrel's technique, but it is hovering nonetheless. Following an autumn east-coast arrival, many of the birds move on and appear to leave Britain, but a few filter further inland to settle in wintering areas which provide open country for feeding as well as enough woodland for secure roosting. The Brecks, downs, and open marshes of the south-east provide such ideal conditions.

55cm

Moorhen
Gallinula chloropus

Coot
Fulica atra

Here are two familiar species, both of which are widespread, common, and present throughout the year. Yet birdwatchers often seem to confuse the two birds. The immediate visual differences are that the Coot is all black (or at least a dark, sooty grey) with a white bill and frontal shield on the forehead. The Moorhen has more contrast in its plumage with shades of brown and green, and it shows white under the tail and has a line on the flanks. The Moorhen's bill is yellow and red and the frontal shield is red. Both are water birds, but again there are subtle differences. The Coot is more a bird of the open, larger areas of water, and spends more time swimming and diving for food, so that its feet are adapted for this purpose by having fleshy lobes on the sides of each toe to make swimming more efficient. The Moorhen prefers the water margins, ditches, and marshes where it spends a considerable amount of time walking over soft ground. The toes are extremely long to distribute its weight over the widest possible area. It would not be correct to assume, however, that Coots do not leave the water or that Moorhens never swim. Grazing flocks of Coot, sometimes several hundred strong, can be a threat to cereal crops or growing grass but, in all situations, they prefer a clear, safe escape route back to the open water. When swimming on open water, the Moorhen shows a distinctive jerking movement with its head and a flicking action of its tail which displays the white under-tail coverts to the best advantage. A very heavy rainstorm is likely to encourage Moorhens out on to the water. The Coot obtains its food by diving whereas the Moorhen is more of a picker and prober. When threatened, however, a Moorhen will often submerge to escape detection, holding itself beneath the surface by grasping some underwater weed, with only the tip of its bill exposed. Both species can become extremely tame when in close proximity to man, and, on town and village ponds, they will readily accept bread from the hand, behaving as boldly as the tamest duck or pigeon. Of the two, though, the Coot is much more quarrelsome and pugnacious. They often hold clearly defined territories which they defend with much fighting and chasing, usually with other Coots but occasionally involving any species that approaches too closely. Although neither of these two species seems to be particularly strong fliers, both are at least partial migrants showing some southerly movement for the winter months. At these times, they are especially susceptible to flying into overhead power lines, and Coots have been recorded from aircraft flying at altitudes of hundreds of metres.

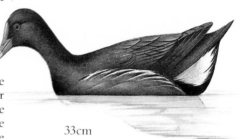

33cm

38cm

Purple Sandpiper

Calidris maritima

An arctic breeding species, the Purple Sandpiper regularly winters further north than any other wader, reaching as far as the ice zone on both sides of the Atlantic. Winter visitors to Britain, the birds arrive each autumn from late October onwards and, by mid-November, most of the wintering quarters hold a large proportion of their birds. Being very much a northern species, Purple Sandpipers arrive in Britain via the northern isles, with Shetland (OS maps 1 to 4) holding nearly 20 per cent of the British population which could well number more than 20 000 birds. Unlike so many of the wintering waders, this is not a bird of the open beaches and mudflats, but an inhabitant of the sea-weed-covered rocks and harbour walls which it frequently shares with the Turnstone. Rarely occurring in large flocks, the birds are usually seen singly or in small parties but are often very difficult to pick out because the dark plumage blends well with the drying seaweed. The Purple Sandpiper is slightly larger than the more familiar Dunlin, and its rather stocky body is carried on yellow legs, which are among its few features to be visible at any distance. A yellow base to the bill, white throat, and eye ring are all apparent at closer range and fortunately, very close approaches can usually be made because the bird shows little fear of man.

21 cm

Grey Phalarope

Phalaropus fulicarius

Each autumn, the Grey Phalarope follows an oceanic route to its wintering grounds. Deserting its breeding sites in the arctic areas on both sides of the Atlantic, the movement southwards takes place far out to sea to its winter destinations in the south Atlantic area; the European populations settle off the African coast whereas the birds from North America remain closer to the western coastline. Although it is a very small wader, Grey Phalaropes still remain in a very hostile environment and they are only rarely seen from the shore, even on the westernmost coast of Ireland. Highly adapted to a marine existence, this small bird will readily settle on the sea during the roughest of conditions. In occasional autumns, however, and particularly following extremely severe western gales, the migrating birds are blown off course and forced to move eastwards to reach sites far from either of the normal migration routes. At such times large flocks may appear on the coastline and in the harbours of south-west Ireland or at souther-westerly sites such as the Isles of Scilly; individuals may even progress the length of the English Channel or penetrate the North Sea. Exceptional years will sometimes produce inland records from gravel pits and reservoirs. Migrating Red-necked Phalaropes which are rather similar to the Grey have usually passed through earlier in the autumn or in late summer and the Grey differs in having a rather shorter, stouter bill, a thicker neck, and a less patterned back.

21 cm

Kingfisher

Alcedo atthis

Rather sparsely distributed in Scotland, the Kingfisher occurs elsewhere in Britain largely as a resident species closely associated with water. Although it will occasionally occur on faster-flowing streams, especially in more upland areas, it is principally a bird of slow-moving or stagnant waters such as reservoirs, gravel pits, or quiet backwaters off the faster-flowing main river. Because it is such a specialized feeder, diving from a convenient perch directly into the water and often completely submerging to catch its prey of small fishes, this bird is highly susceptible to periods of cold weather when water areas become completely frozen over. Water pollution can also seriously affect population levels, although recovery can be rapid because three separate broods in a season are not unusual. In late autumn, a small, post-breeding dispersal can take place, often including a tendency for the birds to move towards the coast. This is probably a means of survival because seawater rarely freezes. At such times a feeding bird will fish from seaweed-covered rocks in much the same manner as it would use an overhanging branch in the more usual freshwater situation. Where convenient perches are lacking, however, the bird will hover before diving. What is perhaps even more unusual about these movements in late autumn is that occasional individuals are found dead at lighthouses at such widely separated sites as Norfolk, Kent, and Ireland.

17cm

Skylark

Alauda arvensis

The Skylark is one of the commonest and most widely spread breeding birds of Britain with an estimated population of some three to four million pairs nesting each year from the northernmost Scottish islands to western Ireland and south-west England. Each November a marked immigration takes place as large numbers from the colder areas of mainland Europe move westwards to the milder maritime climate of Britain. At this time large flocks, often numbering several hundred, can be seen in open country, frequently favouring the ploughed fields with the newly sown cereal crops, or the open downs and heaths. Even though the immigrants are silent, by November, many of the resident birds are again in full song and, although they will again be silenced by extremely cold weather, the Skylark has a very short gap in its annual song period. The highly variable and often con-tinuous outpourings of the singing Skylark are a familiar sound in the British countryside, but many people may be unaware of what the bird looks like. When the bird is walking or running on the ground in a very hunched manner, its streaked brown plumage blends well with its surroundings in open countryside. The crest can frequently be unseen and is often only visible when lifted by the wind. The white outer tail feathers and pale trailing edges to the wings are most apparent as the Skylark takes flight.

18cm

Swallow

Hirundo rustica

The arrival of the Swallow is one of the traditional indications that the British spring is approaching. It is a familiar sight throughout the summer months, frequently living and nesting in close proximity to man. Very few country houses or farms are without a pair of Swallows in the porch, garage, or out-buildings and, in some cases, they can even occur in a small colony usually where a large food supply, attracted by water or livestock, is in the vicinity. By November, the summer is over and very few indeed are the summer migrants that are still with us. To the surprise of many, however, it is not unusual to see a Swallow in November; indeed, in southern England an early December Swallow is reasonably frequent. The majority has, of course, departed, and massive daytime movements in a south-easterly direction throughout September and October have set them off on their annual journey to the southernmost limits of Africa. There they will mingle with Swallows from eastern Europe having leap-frogged past those birds remaining in the more tropical regions. Even the late-departing November individuals will make this long journey for, unlike so many of the insect-eating migrants, Swallows are aerial feeders, that are able to obtain their food while they actively migrate.

19cm

Bearded Tit

Panurus biarmicus

Historically, the Bearded Tit inhabited most of the reed beds in wetland eastern England. The progressive drainage, followed by hard winters dramatically restricted the population until, by the early 1900s, it was a comparatively rare species confined to the Norfolk Broads and very few other sites. Highly specific to the reed-bed habitat, these charming little birds were decimated by the severe winter of 1946–47 when freezing conditions reduced the west European population to perhaps as few as 100 pairs. Since then, steadily increasing numbers resulting from a succession of mild winters have produced quite large-scale post-breeding dispersals which have led to the colonization of reed beds in many parts of the country. November activity is now quite high at most sites where breeding occurs, and observers can expect to encounter the species at such widely spread RSPB reserves as Radipole, Dorset (OS map 194), Titchwell, Norfolk (OS map 132), Blacktoft Sands, Humberside (OS map 112) and Leighton Moss, Lancashire (OS map 97). The bird's striking appearance of warm brown with a grey head and long tail, plus the black moustachial streaks of the male, and very specific choice of habitat have resulted in the wide range of names from 'Reed Pheasant' or 'Water Pheasant' to 'Bearded Reedling'.

16·5cm

Fieldfare

Turdus pilaris

The Fieldfare is larger than the other winter-visiting thrush, the Redwing *(Turdus iliacus)*. It breeds in small numbers in scattered localities, and this is probably part of the slow westward spread of the bird throughout Europe. Still predominantly an immigrant species from Scandinavia, many of the migrants pass through Britain to winter further south and west although large numbers remain to inhabit the farmland fields and hedgerows where, for much of their stay, they exploit insect food on the ground and berries on the bushes. November is the month of peak arrivals and, if the weather pattern over the North Sea or Scandinavian coast is just right with offshore winds and perhaps some cloud and rain at sea, massive migratory arrivals can take place anywhere between Shetland and Kent. Favoured watching points such as Fair Isle, Shetland (OS map 4), Spurn Point, Humberside (OS map 113), or Dungeness, Kent (OS map 189) can record the arrival of many hundreds or even thousands in a single day. The birds seem to tumble from the sky, their harsh chattering calls mingling with the voices of numerous other thrushes. From these coastal arrival points, the movement is onward and frequently inland to the more permanent winter quarters but, even here, the birds can easily be dispersed and forced to undertake further migrations if the weather becomes extremely cold.

25·5cm

Song Thrush

Turdus philomelos

A common and extremely familiar garden bird, the Song Thrush can be seen in Britain throughout the year but, hidden under the appearance of permanent presence, is a complicated migratory pattern. Following the breeding season and up until late October, nearly half the British breeding stock, apparently mostly females, moves westwards and southwards into Ireland, France, and northern Spain. From October onwards a far larger number arrives from the east and, together with the other wintering thrushes, they spread across the country from the east coast. Individuals from the Netherlands and Germany remain, while those from the more northern Scandinavian sites pass through and on to Iberia. The Song Thrush engages in one of the best-known feeding behaviours of all – the use of an anvil, such as a large stone or rock upon which snails are broken open to provide a ready meal. Snails are only part of the diet, however, for, at different times of the year, the principal food can vary from worms, eagerly sought on the dawn lawn, to berries and fruit in the autumn. Snails appear to be an emergency ration, exploited when other foods are scarce although, when hunting for snails, Thrushes carry out a most systematic search. Unfortunately, the closely related Blackbird *(T. merula)* will quickly rob a Thrush once the food has been extracted from the shell but it seems unable to break open a snail itself.

23cm

Redwing

Turdus iliacus

The smallest of the thrush group to breed in Europe, the Redwing is most likely to be confused with the Song Thrush but, although small numbers now nest in Britain, it is still principally a winter visitor closely associated with the berry hedges and open farmland. The Redwing differs from the Song Thrush by having a darker back, prominent pale stripe over the eye, and reddish flanks and underwings. The arrival of the autumn Redwings is mostly concentrated in November and is closely associated with that of the other thrushes. Their arrival, however, occurs on two fronts. In the north and west, many of the birds are from Iceland and make for the Irish or Iberian wintering quarters. These are somewhat darker, more heavily streaked, and slightly larger than the Scandinavian birds which make landfall in eastern Britain and subsequently penetrate westward, especially if forced to do so by cold weather. For a bird from more northern areas, this species seems particularly susceptible to cold weather, quickly becoming tame and moving into gardens where it exploits the abundance of food supplied by man. Indeed, the Redwings appear to be among the first species to succumb in times of freezing temperatures. This is one of the very few migrant birds which can completely change its wintering grounds from year to year. Evidence from ringed individuals suggests that a bird wintering in Britain one year may be in Russia, Italy, or even Turkey in a subsequent winter.

21cm

Blackbird

Turdus merula

This astonishingly abundant and familiar species is probably one of the commonest of all the British land birds, with an estimated population in excess of seven million pairs. It is present throughout the country from the northernmost island in the Shetlands to the Isles of Scilly in the south-west. An excellent example of adaptation and exploitation, the Blackbird can be found in virtually every habitat available, ranging from moorland and farmland to parks, gardens, and city centres. The striking all-black plumage of the male with brilliant orange-yellow bill and eye ring are well known, but the young males with the contrasting brown wings and dark bills are a regular if less-noted sighting during the autumn. Females can be mistaken for Song Thrushes, but are darker brown and certainly darker underneath and lacking the pale ground colour with dark spots. Young Blackbirds, only shortly out of the nest, are particularly strongly spotted for the first few weeks and are a common cause of suggested hybrids between the two species. By November large-scale communal roosts have developed, often in company with other thrush species; usually making the most of particularly dense thickets of hawthorn or rhododendron in which up to 2000 Blackbirds have been recorded.

25cm

Grey Wagtail

Motacilla cinerea

By November the Grey Wagtail has deserted its upland breeding areas beside the fast-flowing streams in the north and west of the country to move to the quieter waters of lowland Britain. Here it favours the banks of reservoirs, gravel pits, canals, and flood meadows which continue to provide the necessary insect food throughout the winter months, although excessive cold with protracted frost will force a weather migration that can take the birds out of the British Isles to the warmer climates of western France or Iberia. To be caught by severe weather can have serious consequences on the population. Following the winter of 1962/63 it was estimated that more than 90 per cent of the British breeding population died, the survivors being those that had moved out before it became very cold. At this time of the year it is hard to confuse the Grey Wagtail with the only other wintering species, the Pied Wagtail, because of the yellow on the Grey's under parts and its very long tail. The high-pitched metallic call immediately separates the species, too, as does its habit of flying up into trees when disturbed. This tree perching, very much a feature on the wintering grounds, has considerable survival value for a species which inhabits often very small areas of water, because it can fly to a safe perch from which to watch any intruder or potential predator until it has passed by.

18cm

Starling

Sturnus vulgaris

The Starling must be one of the most familiar of British birds because it is so closely associated with man throughout the year. During November the quite considerable residential population, probably exceeding four million pairs and their young of the year, is swelled by huge numbers of immigrant birds from the Continent. From as far afield as their breeding grounds to the east of Moscow, Starling populations congregate in vast flocks and begin to move westwards across Europe. Deserting the breeding grounds of Scandinavia and Germany, they seek the milder maritime climate of the Atlantic seaboard. If the weather has been good for migration on the Continental coast, but Britain's east coast is cloud covered or misty, Starlings will often arrive low over the sea in flocks numbering several hundreds or even thousands. This spectacle may be seen at any locality on the east or south coast, the flocks passing low over the sea wall to move on inland and join the British birds foraging on farmland or in suburban back gardens. By November the vast communal roosts have also formed. Feeding birds from a wide area often travel several kilometres to roost in huge numbers – even hundreds of thousands – in a convenient wood or reed bed. The centres of cities, such as London or Newcastle, are also exploited in this way where the warmth and the many buildings with suitable ledges provide the ultimate in night-time security.

21·5cm

Reed Bunting
Emberiza schoeniclus

The Reed Bunting is probably the most familiar of all the British buntings, although this may not always have been true for there has been a dramatic change in its behaviour and habitat. As its name suggests, this is a species of water areas, typically associated with the scrub and other vegetation bordering overgrown lakes or reed beds. In recent years, however, there has been an increasing tendency to spread into drier habitats, apparently ousting the closely related Yellowhammer, to the extent that the Reed Bunting is now just as much at home among a cereal crop or dry scrub area as it is in the more traditional wetland sites. Coupled with this spread has been greater association with man for, by November each year and continuing throughout the winter, the Reed Bunting has become a garden visitor exploiting growing amounts of wild bird food put out by householders. Reed Buntings readily hop on to bird tables among the commoner Sparrows and Greenfinches, and gardens many kilometres from water now receive regular visits. Not all of these birds may be of British origin for, although the Reed Bunting is largely resident, some birds do migrate although no one knows from where they come or their ultimate destination. Arrivals in November at east coast migration points, from Dungeness (OS map 189) north to Fair Isle (OS map 4), almost certainly involve continental, perhaps Scandinavian birds, moving west for the winter months.

15cm

Lapland Bunting
Calcarius lapponicus

The Lapland Bunting is a breeding bird of northern Europe from Scandinavia eastwards, and, as a winter visitor to Britain, it is unlikely to appear before November and in greatly varying numbers from year to year. It rarely moves far from suitable coastal habitat, favouring the saltings or scrub areas close to the high-tide line, for this is very much a ground feeder shuffling along rather like a lark. Indeed, individuals will often associate with Skylark flocks feeding on coastal farmland, and the rattling flight call may be the only indication that a Lapland Bunting is present as the flock flies fast and low over the ploughed ground. First arrivals are usually reported from the northern islands. The birds are noted along the entire length of the east coast, although they are generally in smaller numbers further south. In years of peak counts, however, the north Norfolk coast (OS map 132) and the north Kent marshes (OS map 178) may hold many birds. At the same time, during the November migration, individuals may appear at isolated west coast localities, particularly in Ireland or even as far south as the Isles of Scilly (OS map 203). Although the species is absent from Iceland as a breeding bird, it is highly probable that these individuals have made a considerable oceanic flight from the nesting grounds in Greenland.

15cm

DECEMBER

The cold spell has come early this year. Temperatures well below freezing have persisted throughout the day and there is no sign of a thaw, either of the ice that tops the garden pond or the snow that covers the lawn. The local supermarket and pet store have done a roaring trade in bird food and peanuts, and a high proportion of the gardens in the row have their own birdtable and feeding station. There is an assortment of string bags, seed dispensers, coconut shells, window-sill attachments, and so on. The birds of the area need have no fear of running short of food. Each morning a helpful person breaks the ice on the pond – birds must continue to drink – and clears a patch of snow to reveal the grass beneath. It is here that the ground feeders, the Dunnocks, Robins, and thrushes can obtain food, for not all birds are acrobatic enough to obtain food from the feeding devices arrayed above them. Similarly, not all birds require the commercial bird food – a piece of fruit will be eagerly eaten, with a cut apple perhaps the favourite. An established winter feeding station in the back garden can provide hours of interest for the housebound birdwatcher as the different species react in different ways. The commonest and most expected visitors will be the tits, with both Blue and Great in abundance, but several other species have learnt to adapt, with Greenfinches, House Sparrows, and Starlings all clinging upside-down to feed, if a little clumsily. The Nuthatches have no problems and the peanuts are readily attacked, the slightly larger and heavier bird displacing the tits. However, even the Nuthatch is no match for the Great Spotted Woodpecker should it decide to pay a visit while, in some gardens, it is a never-ending battle to keep the cats at bay or prevent the squirrels emptying the peanuts in a swift foray. Among all this aggression and forceful feeding there will be a few species hovering quietly in the background, never pushing forward, but attracted by the presence of so many birds, The Goldcrests and Treecreepers will be on the fringe of the garden, dependent upon the natural insect food that is still available.

Little Grebe

Tachybaptus ruficollis

Unlike the other grebes, the Little Grebe does not take to a marine habitat during the winter months. Although it forsakes many of the smaller, quieter nesting waters and congregates in quite large numbers on the more open sites, it remains a freshwater species. Only at times of severe weather, when its preferred sites become sheets of ice, will it take to the sea and, even then, it prefers the more sheltered harbours and river mouths to the exposed open beaches. This is one of the most secretive of the grebes, preferring vegetated waters which provide cover in which to hide when the bird is disturbed. The distinctive rounded, rather powder-puff-shaped bird will dive at the first indication of approaching danger and surface within cover where it remains quietly out of sight until all disturbance has passed. This familiar bird is a widespread British species, and is found over a greater geographical range than any other grebe, throughout Europe and much of Asia as far as the Pacific coast, as well as much of Africa and the Pacific islands as far south as New Guinea. Watching our own Little Grebe or Dabchick on the local gravel pit or reservoir, it is hárd to imagine members of the same species on a tropical pool in equatorial New Guinea!

27cm

Pintail

Anas acuta

The British Isles are very much the western fringes of the Pintail's breeding range, with a total nesting population of less than fifty pairs widely scattered throughout the country but concentrated slightly in the eastern counties. During the winter months, however, a large-scale westward and southward movement of Pintails takes place with many birds leaving their east European breeding grounds to cross into Africa. In Britain, the small summer population is steadily increased until, by December, as many as 30 000 birds are present, although they tend to concentrate in specific areas. This figure represents nearly half of the total population wintering in north-west Europe. By far the largest numbers at this time are to be found on the estuary of the River Mersey (OS map 108). Although the species will feed on flooded inland sites, and concentrations of as many as 3000 have been recorded at the Ouse Washes, Cambridgeshire (OS map 143), the Pintail favours the estuaries, using its long neck to graze on underwater vegetation beyond the reach of the smaller ducks. A rather delicate species, its long, thin neck and pointed tail give it a highly distinctive silhouette which makes the flying Pintail immediately identifiable. The plumage of the male is a rather soft grey colour while the female, which also has the thin neck and pointed tail, is a uniform pale, almost creamy brown colour.

60cm

Smew

Mergus albellus

The Smew is one of our smallest and least common wintering ducks. It is completely absent from Britain in the summer months when the entire population is in northern Russia and Asia, where there is little known of its breeding density. As far as Britain is concerned, a December total will rarely reach 200 individuals. In the mid 1900s, a winter birdwatching expedition to any of the London reservoirs in Essex, Middlesex, or Surrey would have encountered reasonable flocks of Smew at all sites and as many as 100 in a single flock would not have been unusual. In recent years a marked decline has taken place and a party reaching double figures is the exception rather than the rule. Only at a very few sites, and the RSPB reserve at Dungeness, Kent (OS map 189) has been one, are Smew numbers regularly present. The unmistakable male in immaculate black-and-white plumage contrasts markedly with the female and young, known as 'redheads' from their chestnut crowns. The decidedly capped appearance of these birds, with their very white face and small size, makes them look rather like smaller grebes in winter plumage – a trap for the unwary. They are diving ducks but they remain submerged for a few seconds only – a short period compared with the longer dives of most of the other species. They feed primarily on free-swimming prey just below the surface.

40cm

Whooper Swan

Cygnus cygnus

In Britain, Mute Swans are familiar birds found on town ponds and rivers, gracefully swimming by with gently curving neck, or rapidly approaching with wings raised to chase away duck or Coot that may be competing for the ready supply of bread. Not so the wild Whooper Swan which leaves its breeding grounds in Iceland, Scandinavia, and northern Russia each autumn and journeys to the Atlantic seaboard of western Europe for the winter. By December wintering flocks are established in their traditional quarters. Although a small number of Icelandic birds remain there for the winter, the majority moves into Britain which holds the remainder of that population, mostly in Ireland and western Scotland with just a few birds finding their way further south to join flocks of the commoner Bewick's Swan *(C. columbianus)*. The largest coastal population in England is near Holy Island (OS map 75) and another regular winter flock can be found at the RSPB reserve at Loch of Strathbeg (OS map 30). Larger than the Bewick's Swan, the Whooper is comparable with the familiar Mute in size but lacks its bulk and usually carries its neck very straight. Compared with that of the smaller Bewick's Swan, the patterning on the bill is distinctive with the yellow extending forward to form a point on the somewhat larger bill. This effect is enhanced by the flatter head.

150cm

Bewick's Swan

Cygnus columbianus

Bewick's Swan is smaller than the other two swan species. It migrates from its arctic Russian breeding grounds to specific sites in western Europe. Nearly one-third of the total number wintering in north-west Europe – more than 2000 birds – can be found in Britain. Two of the best-known, most well-established wintering areas, where large herds of these wild swans can be seen without difficulty, are at the Wildfowl Trust centres at the Ouse Washes, Norfolk (OS map 143) and Slimbridge, Gloucestershire (OS map 162). Both sites have excellent viewing facilities where the species can be examined in close comparison with the other swans as well as with many other wildfowl. At both localities the birds regularly feed on wheat that is provided daily, and birds from arctic regions, where they would normally not come into contact with man, have learnt to accept food as well as feeding in close association with him even to the extent of continuing a normal routine after dark under powerful floodlights. Consequently, it has been possible to study in great detail individual Bewick's Swans. It was discovered that the bill pattern, with its combination of black and yellow, varied in small but highly distinctive ways enabling each bird to be recognized individually. Therefore, the year-by-year pattern of the bird's behaviour and breeding success could be recorded.

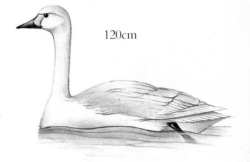

120cm

Capercaillie

Tetrao urogallus

In the early 1800s a winter search of the Scottish pinewoods for Capercaillie would have been unsuccessful. Capercaillies were once widespread throughout much of Scotland and Ireland but the massive tree felling operations among the native pines brought the species to the verge of extinction – an extinction that was finally achieved by pressure from shooting. A re-introduction programme in the latter half of the nineteenth century, using birds of Swedish origin, proved successful and was greatly aided by the steadily increasing afforestation programme in much of central and eastern Scotland. This gigantic member of the grouse family is perhaps somewhat out of place among the pine trees but early on a December morning the Capercaillie can provide a most inspiring sight as it strides majestically beside the pine-fringed road at a site such as the RSPB reserve at Loch Garten (OS map 36). In flight, the bulk of the 4-kilogram male is no less impressive as it crashes out from among the vegetation. Towards the end of December, if the weather is reasonably mild, the males may start their displays together with some astonishing vocal accompaniment. One of the most striking calls sounds remarkably like a cork being withdrawn from a bottle followed by the sound of liquid being poured.

male 85cm   female 60cm

Sanderling

Calidris alba

The Sanderling is a winter visitor to Britain and the complete population has arrived by December. Many of the earlier birds to arrive are passage migrants making their way further south, stopping temporarily on British beaches to refuel for the onward flight to the Mediterranean or African wintering grounds. The numbers of these passage migrants greatly exceed the numbers that eventually winter in Britain. The birds leaving their Siberian and Greenland nesting grounds provide peak numbers in July on their journey south and in May on the journey north. The wintering birds, striking in their very white plumage, compared with the red breeding coloration, originate from both these populations, the Greenland birds favouring the west coast, the Siberian birds in the east. One bird, bearing a coloured ring placed on its leg in Greenland, was recorded for three successive winters in the Isles of Scilly (OS map 203), a site which provides the typical sandy beaches favoured by the species. Although they may occasionally be found in mixed parties with other waders, Sanderlings seem to prefer their own company and have developed a highly distinctive feeding technique. Working close to the water's edge, their twinkling black legs carry them rapidly along the beach rather like little clockwork toys, dashing in and out after each wave rapidly pecking up any small food item deposited by the retreating water.

20cm

Avocet

Recurvirostra avosetta

It is not surprising that the Avocet was chosen as the symbol of the RSPB, for it is a good example of a British bird whose population has become established and has spread as a direct result of conservation work by the Society. In the early years of the nineteenth century, Avocets were probably very widespread among the low-lying coastal marshes of east and south-east England but, by the end of that century, the species seems to have been lost as a British breeding bird, for reasons not fully understood. Occasional nesting attempts in the 1940s were followed by colonization at two sites in Suffolk, Minsmere and Havergate Island (OS map 156), both now well-established reserves of the RSPB. Careful wardening and management of these sites have led to a steadily increasing population which has now spread to sites on the Norfolk coast, and a thriving British breeding population exists again. A further change has also taken place for, at one time, the species was simply a summer visitor and, in those early years of recolonization, observers would await each mid-April with bated breath, never sure if the rather small population of birds would return again. Now a regular wintering population has been established, firstly on the Tamar Estuary, Devon (OS map 201) and, perhaps more surprisingly, an increasing population is now starting to winter on the Havergate breeding grounds.

45cm

Glaucous Gull
Larus hyperboreus

Iceland Gull
L. glaucoides

Both these species of 'white-winged' gulls are winter visitors to Britain, and originate from northern or high-arctic breeding grounds. The Iceland Gull is by far the scarcer of the two, confined to Greenland for its nesting sites whereas the Glaucous Gull is circumpolar. The wider breeding distribution of the latter is also reflected on the British wintering grounds with the slightly larger and heavier Glaucous Gull being the commoner of the two and usually more widely distributed. Both species remain virtually coastal throughout the winter months although occasional Glaucous Gulls may appear at inland gull roosts on some of the larger reservoirs. Both, however, are most likely to be encountered at northern or Irish sites, with many of the harbours in Scotland holding a small but regular wintering population of Glaucous Gulls. Some of these individuals, if immature, may remain throughout the summer rather than return to more northern sites. Occasional birds, which arrive at unexpected beaches, may continue to return for many successive years, indicating just how long lived these large gulls can be. The most distinctive feature of the adult of both species is the very white appearance with no black in the wings or tail feathers, a feature that occurs in no other British gull. An identification note of warning, however; albino examples of both the Herring and Great Black-backed Gulls can occur and, on the Icelandic nesting grounds, hybrids between Glaucous and Herring Gulls are apparently not unusual. It must not be assumed, therefore, that an all-white gull must be either a Glaucous or Iceland Gull. An observer unfamiliar with both species may be forgiven for finding it difficult to decide which one he or she is looking at when, on a December day, one of the two is encountered at a favourite birdwatching site. The Glaucous Gull is a big, heavy, chunky bird with a remarkably thick neck, heavy head, and large bill. In flight its body looks thick set and the wings seem very broad, particularly at the base, and very rounded at the tip. It is a heavyweight prize fighter of the gull world! By comparison, the Iceland Gull is of more delicate appearance. The bill is smaller, less bulbous and set on a smaller head, while the slimmer body appears longer and more tapering. Certainly it is no more than a middleweight or, at the most, a light-heavyweight! In immature plumages, the structural differences remain and still the birds lack any black, but the overall whiteness is replaced with a uniform, pale-brown, slightly greyish plumage, perhaps best likened to a very weak milky coffee colour.

76cm

56cm

Collared Dove

Streptopelia decaocto

The story of the Collared Dove in Britain is quite unique for, within a period of some thirty years, the species has changed its status from being unrecorded in the British Isles to that of a pest species which can be controlled quite legally. This remarkable change goes back to the 1930s when in Europe the species was confined to the south-east, in the Balkans and Turkey. During that decade the bird, which was previously highly sedentary, began to expand its range in a north-westerly direction throughout most of Europe. What was probably the first British record occurred in Lincolnshire in 1952 and, only three years later, the first nesting was recorded at Cromer in Norfolk. Subsequent colonization by the species then became an explosion. From the very first nesting pair the continued spread produced some 3000 pairs in 1964 (only nine years later) and as many as 25 000 pairs by 1970 (only fifteen years after the first nesting). The present-day population could well be more than double this figure, and the species certainly nests in every county in the British Isles. This is a bird that has successfully exploited a close association with man. Initially, it was with his farming activities, and the largest concentration of Collared Doves were to be found around the grain stores, livestock pens, and chicken farms but, as the population continued to increase, gardens, parks, and city centres were also invaded, habitats that the birds had exploited in the south-east of Europe before their expansion.

30cm

Lesser Spotted Woodpecker

Dendrocopos minor

The Lesser Spotted Woodpecker is the smallest and least noticeable of the British woodpeckers. Not much bigger than a Sparrow and very much a bird of the tree tops, it can be easily overlooked but winter is perhaps the best time of the year for finding the species. The trees are leafless and small movements in the topmost branches become obvious. The ringing 'ki-ki-ki . . .', which is rather similar to the call of a distant bird of prey or singing Wryneck, will attract attention to the bird and, on warm days from late December onwards, drumming will begin. Drumming is confined to the two spotted woodpeckers and is their equivalent of a song. The bill is tapped rapidly against some dead resonant wood to produce this far-carrying sound. It is not always easy to separate the drumming of the two species, but the Lesser Spotted's usually lasts longer and is a series of more rapid taps which, when analysed, occur at about fifteen per second as opposed to the Great Spotted's ten. The Lessser Spotted lacks the large white shoulder patch and, as a result, it is also known as the 'Barred Woodpecker' because of the strong white barring on the otherwise black upper parts.

14cm

Great Tit
Parus major

Blue Tit
P. caeruleus

The habit of feeding garden birds has now become a major British pastime, to the extent that it supports a minor industry which supplies a whole range of sophisticated devices designed to make watching garden birds more interesting. Tables, feeders, nut holders, and window sill attachments are all readily available as is a wide range of food stuffs, from the standard peanuts and coconuts to specially prepared mixtures which include suitable items for many species. Whenever Britain experiences a cold winter, more and more people wish to feed birds so that their rural and surburban gardens become established as feeding stations. Without doubt, the commonest feeding technique is to hang peanut kernels in orange string bags – and the commonest birds to be attracted to this food source are the Blue and Great Tits in that order of abundance. The natural agility of feeding tits, hanging from the outermost foliage of trees where they search for insect food on the undersides of leaves and among the buds, has made them ideally suited to hang from peanut containers, and it seems quite natural for them to spend much of their lives upside down. Many garden birds, however, are great opportunists and the sight of a bird obtaining food leads them to imitate and attempt similar exploitation. No other species has quite the same knack as the tits but, among the most successful has been the Greenfinch, while the Siskin also finds no difficulty because of its normal feeding techniques even though it only visits peanut bags occasionally. Sparrows, Starlings, Chaffinches, Robins, and, no doubt, a few others have also made use of this now regular food source but none of these is as agile nor gives as much pleasure to the bird gardener as do these two species of tit. Detailed studies have shown that, in a garden situation where food attracts as many as five or six different Blue Tits at a time, the total number of tits passing through the garden during the day may be as high as thirty or forty different individuals. The larger, bolder Great Tit is usually the more dominant of the two, tending to be a little more quarrelsome and somewhat of a bully. Where supplies are dwindling, the Great Tit is only too ready to chase off other species although, in fact, a little less chasing and more feeding would prove beneficial to all! With regular feeding, many of the birds become very tame, often happily taking food from window ledges and even entering houses. Consequently individuals can be observed very closely and it is soon obvious that no two birds are identical in appearance or behaviour. Great Tits may be easily sexed by the width of the black line down the centre of the under parts, readily seen as the birds hang from the peanut bags. In the males, the black band is broader and spreads between the legs; in the females it remains narrow and thin.

14cm

11·5cm

Coal Tit
Marsh Tit

Parus ater

P. palustris

Coal and Marsh Tits are less familiar to most enthusiastic bird feeders and are confined to the more rural feeding stations. The Coal Tit is found throughout the British Isles except in the northernmost islands and, in many areas, it has a particular liking for the conifer woods. It may still be found in deciduous woodland, however, and in several areas in Ireland and in many of the Scottish birchwoods, it outnumbers all the other tits. The Marsh Tit, by contrast, is a less numerous species, rarely found near conifers, preferring the mixed deciduous woodlands of England and Wales, and especially those with dense shrub cover. Neither species makes itself particularly noticeable when it is at the peanut bag, slipping in quietly, pecking hurriedly, and then moving away at the first signs of any disturbance. Rarely do they contest the food with the dominant and commoner Blue and Great Tits but, the Coal Tit can become the tamest of all the tits and is often the first to venture into a new situation in search of food. At one regular feeding site where Great, Blue, and Coal Tits were almost continually present at peanuts, it was always the Coal Tits that were the first to enter an open window to take any food that was available inside the room. On the other hand, the Marsh Tit is a particularly shy member of the group. Away from gardens in December many of the tits, often mixed with other species, join together in foraging parties moving noisily through the woodland as they systematically search for food items in the crags and crevices of the trees. Although Marsh Tits are rarely the commonest birds, they often appear to be leading the flock and the direction it will travel. With most species, including the tits, the pairs break down in the winter months and the communal flocks are just collections of individuals. The Marsh Tit, however, appears to be an exception in that the pairs often remain together at this time, and their highly distinctive, ringing 'pitchu' call note can be heard coming from the flock. If you watch these different species of tits in their winter flocks you will notice that each seems to concentrate its searching in a particular part of the wood. The Great Tit is most often on the lower branches or even on the ground; the Blue Tit is higher in the tree and rarely comes to ground level; the Coal Tit favours the outer branches of conifers and the trunks of other trees; while the Marsh Tit is very much a bird of the lower scrub vegetation rather than the trees themselves.

11·5cm

11·5cm

Willow Tit

Parus montanus

Superficially resembling the Marsh Tit, the Willow Tit can often be overlooked by the inexperienced birdwatcher. The bird's name does not adequately suggest its preferred habitat for, just as the Marsh Tit has no close association with marshes, the Willow Tit has no direct connection with willows. Indeed, of the two species, it is the Willow Tit that is more likely to inhabit wet areas or sites near open water although, in many places, both will often breed in the same wood. They have similar distributions, too, although the Willow Tit is found a little further north, inhabiting southern Scotland. The Willow Tit has a dull, sooty cap rather than the bright, glossy black one of the Marsh Tit. Overall, it is greyer in appearance and has pale edges to the flight feathers which form a definite patch on the closed wing. The Willow Tit is rather whiter on the under parts and has a slightly larger black bib so that, in general, it looks untidier than the sleeker-looking Marsh Tit. Two other features, voice and nesting habits, are distinctive. The Willow Tit is rarely as vocal as the Marsh, but it will make a series of slightly buzzing notes as well as the more usual harsh nasal calls that are so typical of the species. Both species are hole nesting but, whereas the Marsh Tit will accept a ready made site, including a nest box, the Willow Tit prefers to excavate its own nesting cavity.

11·5cm

Nuthatch

Sitta europaea

The Nuthatch is very much a bird of the mature woodlands of England and Wales and, on a December day, the distinctive but highly variable and far-carrying whistling call can be heard originating from the topmost branches of some gigantic beech or oak. The most typical, clear whistle is remarkably human-like, in some ways reminiscent of a ringing 'wolf whistle'. Although it is principally an insect feeder, the bird's name originates from the aggressive manner in which it will obtain the kernel from any nut that is discovered during its foraging. The nut is firmly wedged in a crack or crevice, usually one that is used regularly for this purpose, and then attacked with short, sharp blows, the noise of which can be heard some considerable distance away. At intervals, the nut is removed, turned or examined, and then replaced to be attacked from a different angle. At such times the bird often uses its feet to help hold the nut, and it is remarkable how it manages to avoid striking its own toes. When foraging, the Nuthatch moves through the trees with considerable agility, perching in the normal manner of any small bird as well as hopping along the vertical surfaces of the trunk or the undersides of a branch. Unlike woodpeckers or Treecreepers (*Certhia familiaris*) Nuthatches rely entirely upon their feet, the short tail offering no support. But, whereas the other species can only climb steadily upwards sitting on their tails, the Nuthatch can move up or down and even jump sideways.

14cm

Treecreeper
Certhia familiaris

Only absent from the northernmost islands, the resident Treecreeper is a rather secretive and certainly much overlooked bird. Although it will join winter tit flocks, and occurs in gardens and open parkland, it is most at home in some of our densest woodland. Keeping extremely close to the trunks and main branches, and often appearing always to be on the other side of the tree from the observer, it moves steadily upwards in little jerky runs, its brown-patterned plumage blending superbly with the background. Appropriately, it has often been described as behaving in a mouse-like manner. Even the rather thin, high-pitched calls are not likely to draw attention to the bird and its somewhat weak song lacks carrying power although it can be heard on almost any fine day even in the midst of winter. Regularly encountered in village woods or churchyards, the species has acquired numerous local names such as the 'tree climber' or 'bark runner' most of which have obvious derivations, but the origin of 'eeckle', 'cuddy', or 'daddy-ike' must remain a mystery. For food the Treecreeper relies entirely on insects using its long, decurved bill to discover the overwintering insects tucked into crevices or beneath the bark that birds with shorter or stouter bills cannot reach. Frequently associating with the winter tit flocks, the Treecreeper usually follows behind, apparently happy to be led around by the other species.

12·5cm

Stonechat
Saxicola torquata

By December the Stonechats have long deserted their heather- and gorse-clad nesting sites. Many of the British breeding birds have migrated southwards to spend the winter in the Mediterranean region, but not all depart our shores, and their numbers may well be swelled by immigrant Stonechats from northern Europe. The winter distribution has a decidedly coastal flavour, with saltmarshes and sea walls providing homes, although these areas will quickly be deserted if there is any prolonged freezing weather. At these times a marked southerly and westerly movement takes place, and much of eastern England loses its Stonechats for the remainder of the winter. On the wintering grounds a definite territory is established and birds will remain in pairs on the same site throughout. Consequently, once a wintering bird of either sex has been located, the mate will soon be revealed. The sexes are easily distinguished, the male showing the striking black head and contrasting white collar. The female is a much drabber version but retains the characteristic stance, with its rather large head on a rounded body with short tail and long legs. The most typical behaviour is to perch in an upright position on the top of convenient vegetation or fence flicking its wings. From here it can easily drop to the ground to collect its food.

12·5cm

Goldcrest

Regulus regulus

The smallest of the British birds, the Goldcrest weighs only a little over 5 grams and yet it will readily undertake a considerable migration. At a little over 50 millimetres, the Goldcrest's wing is longer than that of the Wren, which is some 5 millimetres or more shorter, but the Wren is a bulkier bird with a weight of over 9 grams. These two birds provide a good example of adaptive development – the non-migratory Wren is heavier and shorter winged than the migratory Goldcrest. Every autumn large numbers of Goldcrests move south out of Scandinavia, and birds move westwards out of eastern Europe. These tiny birds undertake a twice-annual crossing of the southern North Sea – and not always do things go quite right. Sudden bad weather, heavy cloud, rain, or freshening winds when the journey is half completed can send them astray and many may die. There are numerous records of flocks of Goldcrests descending upon light vessels or oil rigs. But every year large numbers successfully make the journey although it was once thought that they hitch-hiked on the backs of Short-eared Owls which arrive in eastern England at much the same time. By December the birds are dispersed into the woods and parklands over much of Britain, although they are scarcer in the north. Frequently, they associate with foraging flocks of tits, Nuthatches, and Treecreepers, adding their extremely thin, high-pitched contact call to the general noise of the mixed party.

9cm

Twite

Carduelis flavirostris

A breeding bird of the Highlands of northern Scotland, the Twite has been well named the 'Mountain Linnet' for it very much replaces that species in the upland areas. Such sites are completely inhospitable in the winter months and, by December, they are completely deserted and the birds are established in their winter quarters which are in complete contrast to the nesting areas. From mountains the birds move to sea-level (although in some northern sites they nest by coastal cliffs) and they exchange the heather, which seems to be an important part of the summer habitat, for the saltmarsh and its associated vegetation of river estuaries. The feeding patterns at these times are often dictated by the tides, flocks having to move off the saltmarsh in front of the advancing water. They often form mixed flocks with the wintering Linnets and the first confirmation that Twite are present is often the double nasal flight call. Observers looking at Twite on the ground should note the yellow bill, pinkish rump, especially in the male, and the clear unmarked throat. The December birdwatcher can expect to find a regular wintering flock of Twite near the mouth of the River Blackwater, Essex (OS map 168).

13·5cm

Birds through the year

In the following charts, all the birds described in the *Calendar* are listed in alphabetical order, noting the page on which a description of the bird can be found. In the centre column of the chart, the months of the year during which each bird's four major phases of activity occur are shown by lines as follows:

spring migration ▮▮▮▮▮▮▮▮▮▮▮▮▮▮▮▮▮▮▮▮   autumn migration �

breeding ░░░░░░░░░░░░░░   wintering ▒▒▒▒▒▒▒▒

If a line is broken further, then that phase is uncertain.
In the right-hand column, the habitats in which each species might be found are indicated by the following symbols:

woodlands 🌳   uplands ⛰

coast 〰   lakes and rivers 〰

marsh ░   farmland 🌾

heaths ░   towns and gardens 🏠

For those birds that breed in Britain, their distribution during breeding is also given.

Species	Jan Feb Mar Apr May June July Aug Sep Oct Nov Dec	Habitat & Distribution
Arctic Skua p93		〰 N & W Scotland
Arctic Tern p83		〰 Scotland & Ireland patchy England & Wales
Avocet p154		〰 E England
Barn Owl p64		🌾 🌳 ░ England & Wales, patchy Scotland & Ireland
Barnacle Goose p50		〰 ░ 🌾

Species	Jan Feb Mar Apr May June July Aug Sep Oct Nov Dec	Habitat & Distribution
Bar-tailed Godwit p72		
Bean Goose p41		
Bearded Tit p145		S & E England
Bewick's Swan p153		
Bittern p69		E England, patchy W England
Black Grouse p51		Scotland, Wales, N England patchy SW England
Black Guillemot p96		N & W Scotland, Ireland patchy NW England & Wales
Black Redstart p66		SE England
Black Tern p125		
Blackbird p147		throughout Britain
Blackcap p47		England, Wales, S Scotland patchy N Scotland & Ireland
Black-headed Gull p94		N England, Wales, Scotland & Ireland patchy S & E England

Species	Jan Feb Mar Apr May June July Aug Sep Oct Nov Dec	Habitat & Distribution
Black-necked Grebe p110		patchy Scotland
Black-tailed Godwit p72		patchy, S & E England
Blue Tit p157		throughout Britain
Brambling p138		throughout Britain
Brent Goose p41		
Bullfinch p128		throughout Britain
Buzzard p102		Scotland, Wales, N Ireland & W England
Canada Goose p101		England, patchy elsewhere
Capercaillie p153		Scotland
Carrion Crow p54		throughout Britain
Cetti's Warbler p135		SE England
Chaffinch p138		throughout Britain

Species	Jan Feb Mar Apr May June July Aug Sep Oct Nov Dec	Habitat & Distribution
Chiffchaff p46		England, Wales, S Scotland, Ireland patchy N Scotland
Chough p117		Wales, Ireland, Isle-of-Man patchy W Scotland
Cirl Bunting p67		SW England
Collared Dove p156		throughout Britain
Common Gull p63		Scotland, N Ireland
Common Sandpiper p123		N England, Wales, Scotland, W Ireland
Common Scoter p79		patchy Scotland & Ireland
Common Tern p115		N & SE England, Scotland, Ireland, Anglesey
Coal Tit p158		throughout Britain
Coot p142		throughout Britain
Cormorant p100		W England, Wales, W Scotland, Ireland
Corn Bunting p98		England, E Scotland

Species	Jan Feb Mar Apr May June July Aug Sep Oct Nov Dec	Habitat & Distribution
Corncrake p92		patchy W Scotland, Ireland
Crested Tit p74		patchy Scotland
Crossbill p108		patchy throughout Britain
Cuckoo p107		throughout Britain
Curlew p103		W England, Wales, Scotland, Ireland
Curlew Sandpiper p124		
Dartford Warbler p67		patchy S England
Dipper p55		N & W England, Wales, Scotland, Ireland
Dunlin p132		patchy N England, Wales, Scotland, Ireland
Dunnock p117		throughout Britain
Eider p69		Scotland, N Ireland
Fieldfare p146		

166

Species	Jan Feb Mar Apr May June July Aug Sep Oct Nov Dec	Habitat & Distribution
Firecrest p128		
Fulmar p59		throughout Britain
Gadwall p39		E England, otherwise patchy
Gannet p90		16 separate colonies
Garden Warbler p86		England & Wales, patchy Scotland, Ireland
Garganey p110		patchy England
Glaucous Gull p155		
Goldcrest p161		throughout Britain
Golden Eagle p70		Scotland
Golden Plover p71		N England & Scotland, patchy Wales & Ireland
Goldeneye p61		patchy Scotland
Goldfinch p77		England, Wales, S Scotland, Ireland

Species	Jan	Feb	Mar	Apr	May	June	July	Aug	Sep	Oct	Nov	Dec	Habitat & Distribution
Goosander p80			▮▮▮▮▮▮▮▮▮ (Mar–May)			▒▒▒▒ (Apr–Aug)				██ (Sep–Nov)		▒ (Jan–Mar); ▒ (Nov–Dec)	≋ N England, Scotland
Goshawk p62				▒▒▒▒ (Apr–Aug)									♣ patchy England & Scotland
Grasshopper Warbler p84			▮▮▮▮▮▮▮▮▮ (Mar–June)			▒▒ (May–July); ██ (June–Sep)							♣ ░░ throughout Britain
Great Black-backed Gull p44				▒▒▒▒ (Apr–Aug)									≋ W England, Wales, Scotland, Ireland
Great Crested Grebe p59				▒▒▒▒ (Apr–Sep)									≋ England, Wales, S Scotland, Ireland
Great Grey Shrike p137		▮▮▮▮▮▮ (Feb–Apr)							██ (Aug–Oct)			▒ (Jan–Mar); ▒ (Oct–Nov)	
Great Northern Diver p79			▮▮▮▮▮ (Mar–May)					██ (July–Oct)				▒ (Jan–Apr); ▒ (Oct–Dec)	
Great Skua p93			▮▮▮▮▮▮▮ (Mar–June)			▒▒ (May–Aug); ██ (June–Sep)							≋ ▲ N Scotland
Great Spotted Woodpecker p74				▒▒▒▒ (Apr–Aug)									♣ England, Wales, Scotland
Great Tit p157				▒▒ (Apr–June)									♣ 🌲 throughout Britain
Green Sandpiper p103			▮▮▮▮▮▮▮▮ (Mar–June); ██ (June–Sep)							▒ (Oct–Nov)			
Green Woodpecker p126				▒▒▒▒ (Apr–Aug)								▒ (Jan–Mar)	♣ England, Wales, S Scotland

Species	Jan Feb Mar Apr May June July Aug Sep Oct Nov Dec	Habitat & Distribution
Greenfinch p137		throughout Britain
Greenshank p113		N Scotland
Grey Phalarope p143		
Grey Plover p113		
Grey Wagtail p148		throughout Britain, patchy England
Greylag Goose p101		patchy throughout Britain
Guillemot p95		W England, Wales, Scotland, Ireland
Hawfinch p56		patchy England, Wales, S Scotland
Hen Harrier p130		patchy N England, Wales, Scotland, Ireland
Heron p49		throughout Britain
Herring Gull p105		throughout Britain
Hobby p80		S England

Species	Jan Feb Mar Apr May June July Aug Sep Oct Nov Dec	Habitat & Distribution
House Martin p134		throughout Britain
House Sparrow p108		throughout Britain
Iceland Gull p155		
Jack Snipe p131		
Jackdaw p134		throughout Britain
Jay p126		England, Wales, S Scotland, Ireland
Kestrel p121		throughout Britain
Kingfisher p144		England, Wales, S Scotland, Ireland
Kittiwake p106		W & N England, Wales Scotland, Ireland
Knot p43		
Lapland Bunting p149		
Lapwing p102		throughout Britain

Species	Jan Feb Mar Apr May June July Aug Sep Oct Nov Dec	Habitat & Distribution
Lesser Black-backed Gull p63		S & W England, Wales, Scotland, Ireland
Lesser Spotted Woodpecker p156		England, Wales
Lesser Whitethroat p77		England, patchy Wales
Linnet p118		throughout Britain patchy N Scotland
Little Grebe p151		throughout Britain
Little Gull p105		
Little Owl p115		England & Wales
Little Ringed Plover p71		England
Little Stint p124		
Little Tern p73		patchy throughout Britain
Long-eared Owl p44		patchy throughout Britain
Long-tailed Tit p66		throughout Britain

Species	Jan Feb Mar Apr May June July Aug Sep Oct Nov Dec	Habitat & Distribution
Magpie p65		England, Wales, S Scotland, Ireland
Mallard p120		throughout Britain
Mandarin Duck p140		
Manx Shearwater p120		W England, Wales, W Scotland, Ireland
Marsh Harrier p91		E England
Marsh Tit p158		England & Wales
Marsh Warbler p85		W England
Meadow Pipit p136		throughout Britain
Mediter-ranean Gull p133		
Merlin p131		N England, Wales, Scotland, Ireland
Mistle Thrush p55		throughout Britain
Moorhen p142		throughout Britain

172